Born at the turn of the twentieth century, in 1900, VIJAYA LAKSHMI PANDIT was the daughter of Motilal Nehru and his second wife, Swaruprani. She played a key role in India's freedom struggle. After Independence, Pandit entered the diplomatic service and served as India's ambassador to the Soviet Union, the United States, Mexico and Ireland. She was also the Indian High Commissioner to the United Kingdom. In 1953, she became the first woman President of the United Nations General Assembly. In India, she served as Governor of Maharashtra from 1962 to 1964, and was elected to the Lok Sabha twice, in 1952 and 1964. Her writings include *So I Became a Minister* (1939) and *The Scope of Happiness: A Personal Memoir* (1979).

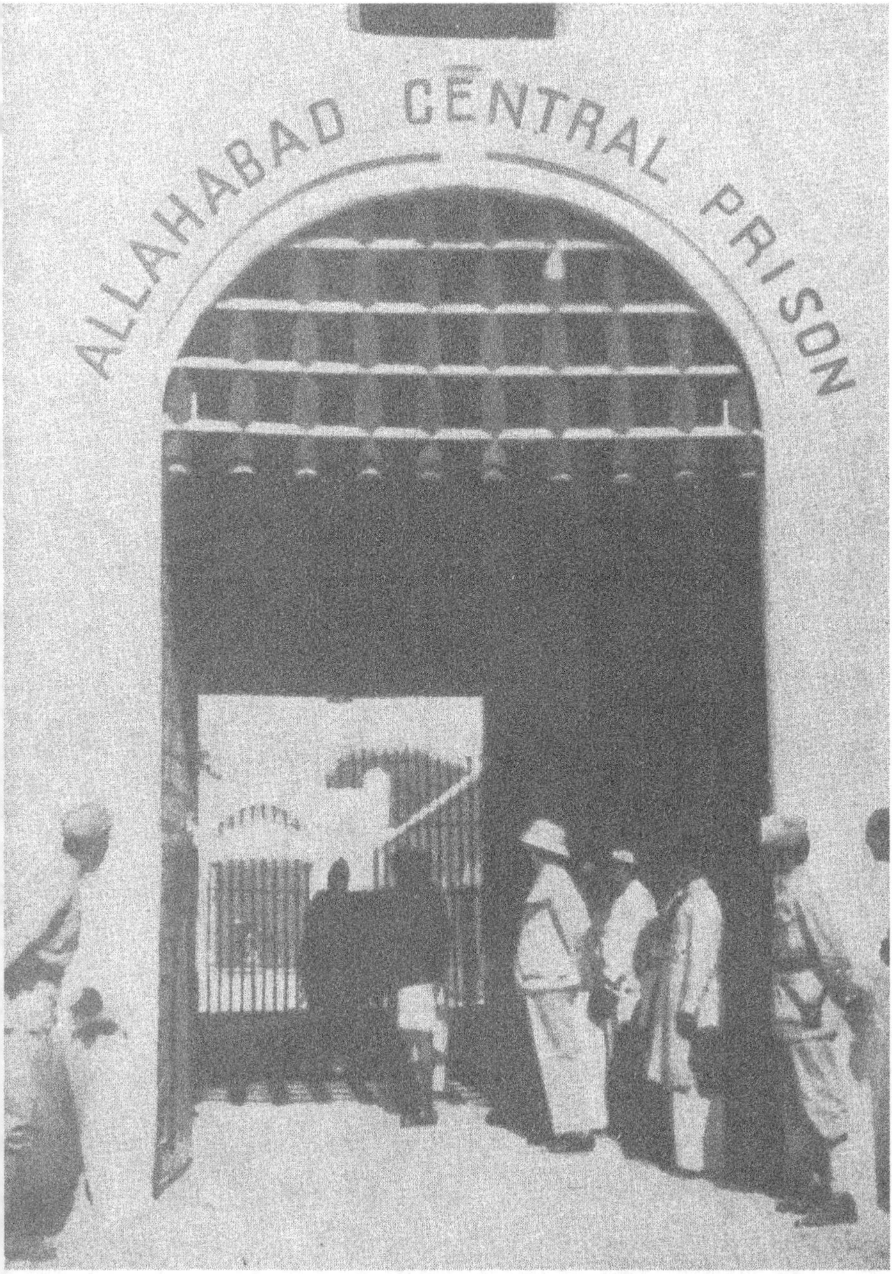
ALLAHABAD CENTRAL PRISON

PRISON DAYS

Vijaya Lakshmi Pandit

SPEAKING TIGER PUBLISHING PVT LTD
4381/4 Ansari Road, Daryaganj,
New Delhi–110002, India

This edition published by Speaking Tiger 2018

Copyright © Nayantara Sahgal, Literary Executor of
the Estate of Vijaya Lakshmi Pandit

ISBN: 978-93-87693-01-2
eISBN: 978-93-87164-81-9

10 9 8 7 6 5 4 3 2 1

The moral right of the author has been asserted.

Typeset in Charter BT by Jojy Philip
Printed at Sanat Printers, Kundli

All rights reserved.
No part of this publication may be reproduced,
transmitted, or stored in a retrieval system, in any form or
by any means, electronic, mechanical, photocopying,
recording or otherwise, without the prior
permission of the publisher.

This book is sold subject to the condition that it shall not,
by way of trade or otherwise, be lent, resold, hired out,
or otherwise circulated, without the publisher's
prior consent, in any form of binding or cover
other than that in which it is published.

To
G.R.O.
in friendship and gratitude

'A day went shyly by—today as yesterday,
A quick and empty drop spilled into time.
When night out of her gathered folds
Strews her last shadow on the dawn's pale way
The light's cold kiss no sweetness holds;
Tomorrow's face is but as yesterday's.'

Foreword

My mother, Vijaya Lakshmi Pandit, wrote this prison diary during her third and last imprisonment under ~~Brtish~~ rule. It begins on 12 August 1942, six days before her forty-second birthday. World War II was on, Allahabad, like the rest of the country, was under military rule. Arrest and imprisonment took place without trial. Several lorries filled with armed policemen arrived that night at Anand Bhawan at 2 a.m. to arrest one lone, unarmed woman, who, along with her husband, Ranjit Sitaram Pandit, and her brother, Jawaharlal Nehru, had committed her life to the non-violent fight to free India from British rule, under the leadership of Mahatma Gandhi.

My father was already a prisoner in Naini Central Jail in Allahabad, where she was taken, and he would later be transferred to jail in Bareilly, where he would fall mortally ill, and finally be released only to die. My uncle was imprisoned 'somewhere in

India'. It was not made public until much later that he and other leaders of the Indian National Congress were held in the Ahmednagar Fort. My older sister, Chandralekha, aged eighteen, and my cousin, Indira Gandhi, aged twenty-five, were arrested later and taken to Naini Jail.

For those who have grown up in independent India, this little diary will give a glimpse of the courage and commitment it took to fight an empire at great cost to themselves and their families. Women played a major role in the fight, tens of thousands of them, known and unknown, suffering the hardships and separations from their loved ones that imprisonment involved. But my mother's diary also shows the refusal to be bowed or broken by this grim experience, and how she, my sister and my cousin—in the same barrack with a dozen or so women convicted for murder and other crimes—made light of it.

– Nayantara Sahgal

Dehradun,
December 2017

Preface

This little diary does not attempt to record all the events which took place during my last term of imprisonment. It was not written regularly and is of no special importance. But since the period from August 1942 onwards was enveloped in darkness and many people still have no idea what prison life means, this may help in giving a picture of the conditions prevailing in one of the better run jails of the United Provinces.

The treatment given to me and to those who shared the barrack with me was, according to the prison standards, very lenient—the reader must not imagine that others were equally well treated. When the truth about that unhappy period is made known many grim stories will come to light, but that time is still far off.

A few pages of the diary and some incidents

have had to be omitted for obvious reasons. I offer this little book to those who are interested in understanding something of what goes on behind the prison gates.

Vijaya Lakshmi Pandit.

Prison Days

12th August 1942

I woke up with a start and switched on the light. Binda was standing at the foot of my bed. He told me the police had arrived and wished to see me. It was 2 a.m. My mind was a confused jumble of the events of the preceding twenty-four hours. The shots fired on the students' procession were still ringing in my ears and before my eyes I could only see the faces of those young men whom I had helped to pick up and remove to hospital. I was utterly weary in mind and body and more than a little dazed.

The girls were asleep on the veranda and I did not wish to disturb them. Both Lekha and Tara had gone to bed exhausted after what they had been through the day before. They had seen sights which would not easily be effaced from their memory and were bewildered and unhappy.

I went out to the porch. The City Magistrate, the Deputy Superintendent of Police, and half a dozen armed policemen were standing waiting for me in the darkness. I switched on the light and was amazed to find the grounds full of plain-clothes men some of whom had actually come up on to the veranda. This annoyed me and very curtly I ordered them off into the garden before speaking to the City Magistrate. He was ill at ease and said he had a warrant for my arrest. 'Why is it necessary for so many armed men to come to arrest one unarmed woman at this amazing hour?' I asked. A search was also to take place, I was informed. I told them to go ahead with the search while I got ready for prison.

I had not expected to be arrested and was taken by surprise. There was no one with the girls, no possibility of making satisfactory arrangements. Indira had arrived from Bombay a few hours earlier. She was tired so I ran upstairs to say goodbye to her. After a kiss and a few hurried instructions to Indira I woke the girls and broke the news. They were brave as always and immediately grasped the situation—no useless questions, no fuss. All three of them helped me to pack and Lekha hurriedly put together a few books for me to take along. Rita looked at me with big eyes heavy with sleep. Looking at her my courage began to ebb. She was so little and the world was so big—who would take care of her? As if sensing my thoughts she smiled at me. 'How wonderful to live in these days, Mummie,' she said, 'I wish I could go to jail too.' I felt suddenly that there was no need to worry and with a lighter heart I bent down to kiss her. 'Let's say goodbye to you outside, Mummie,' Tara said, 'I want the police to see how we take these partings.' They came out with me and in the porch we said goodbye. 'Darling, don't worry. Everything will be fine. I will look after the kids,' said Lekha, giving me a quick tight hug. 'Bye-bye Mummie darling,' said Tara, 'we shall keep the flag flying.' Her eyes were bright and she held her head high. Rita clung to me for a minute but her voice was firm as she said, 'Mummie darling, take care of yourself. We shall be fighting the British outside while you are in.'

By this time some of the servants had arrived and I was able to say goodbye to them. They were not as brave as the children and some of them had tears in their eyes. I walked down the drive to the gate and was surprised to find it locked as was usual at that hour. How had the police come in? Evidently by the side wicket. We went out the same way.

Three or more police lorries were lined up on the road outside. In the darkness I could not make out the exact number. More armed men appeared out of the shadows. I was asked to get into the first lorry. The D.S.P. took the wheel. The City Magistrate and some others got in behind and we started.

The city had been in the hands of the military for several hours—martial law in everything but name and a curfew order in force. We drove in an atmosphere of extreme tension. As we travelled along the familiar road to Naini my mind was full of many thoughts and before my eyes like some film in a cinema were pictures of other journeys—dozens of them from 1921 onwards. We reached the Jumna Bridge, heavily guarded and were challenged by the sentries on duty. Even after the words 'Friend' and 'Police Car' were shouted, the vigilant sentry was doubtful about letting us proceed—what terrific loyalty the British inspire in those who serve them!

Arriving at Naini I was informed that the jail authorities had not been intimated of my approaching arrival. Orders had, apparently, been communicated late at night to the police and the jail staff did not expect me. After a half an hour's wait, the door of the Female Prison was opened and the matron in the manner of all jail matrons, came rushing along panting and puffing and very much out of breath.

I was conducted to the old familiar barrack. It was 3.45 a.m. I spread my bedding on the ground, was locked in, and a new term of prison life began. My head ached badly and the throbbing in my temple prevented sleep. I lay thinking over the events of the past two days. I was worried about Lekha and felt she would land up in prison. The previous evening as she was going to bed I talked with her and tried to get her reactions to events. She spoke with great bitterness, 'It will take a long time for me to forget what I have seen, Mummie, and it will be longer before I can root out the hatred which is growing in my heart. We can't think in terms of normal life any more—there's no going back for us. We must go on straight to the end, whatever the end may be.' Of course she is right—we must go on—to the end. At last I fell asleep.

13th August 1942

My first thought on waking was of the girls. My head continued to ache and I lay in bed until the lambardarni announced that she wished to sweep the barrack.

There are few of the old familiar faces left and the new ones look at me like something out of a museum. There is no water, no sanitary arrangements—in fact nothing at all. I walked in the yard for half an hour, then I got a little water from the convicts' bathing tap and washed my face. About seven the matron came and said she would send me some tea from her house as the jail was unable to supply rations until 10 a.m. I had no desire to accept the matron's tea but my head continued to throb and I thought perhaps the tea would help. It didn't. I spent a miserable day.

Towards noon some raw rations arrived, but still no coal, so cooking was not possible. Later, with the help of one of the convicts, I made a small fire of twigs and made an attempt to cook but it was a failure as the fire would not light. I read and slept and finally got up at 4 p.m. to start this diary. It is now six and lock-up takes place in a few moments.

Here comes the matron followed by the usual

procession of wardresses to lock up and so ends the first day in my third term of imprisonment.

After lock-up the matron came back again in half an hour and announced that she had orders to leave my barrack open and that I might sleep outside if I wished. I was glad of this concession. Before leaving, she enquired what I was having for dinner and was horrified when I said I had nothing to eat at hand. She wanted to send me something but I refused.

I walked in the yard for a while. It was fairly cool and my head felt much better. As I walked I almost forgot that I had been away from here for nearly a year and half. It seemed as if this was just a continuation of the previous imprisonment. I put my bed outside in the yard and lay down to read—but my mind wandered and I could not follow the book. Every now and again shouts of 'Inquilab Zindabad' and other slogans came to me over the wall. I felt less alone after that, and in a way, happier. The stars were out and I lay looking up at the sky for a while, then went back to my book. At 9.30 I put out the light as hoards of insects were making life impossible by crawling all over me and getting into my hair.

I woke up at eleven to find myself wet and the rain coming down in torrents. By the time I had brought my bed in, I was soaked and had to change. After the rain it was cool and I had a peaceful night.

14th August 1942

I woke up in the morning feeling fresh and prepared to be civil to the world, but when by 8.30 a.m. there was no coal and no tea I found myself losing my temper. I think hunger had something to do with it also. The matron had not been, so I wrote and informed the Superintendent that since I had been admitted to the jail no food had been supplied to me and if it had not been for the matron's kindness in sending me some tea from her house I should have starved completely. I mentioned that if the jail was short of raw rations I might be given the cooked food served to the convicts. This note brought the matron running and out of breath—full of apologies for the slackness in the arrival of my rations.

Shortly afterwards some raw rations and vegetables arrived and a bundle of firewood. Earlier I had, with the help of one of the convicts built a chula in the portion of the veranda which is to serve as a kitchen. I cleaned up some vegetables and cooked a simple meal. Being really hungry I enjoyed it.

15th August 1942

Food is an overrated subject. One realizes this most forcibly in jail. It is all right if one is in pleasant surroundings with the right people and the food is well cooked and well served. It is certainly possible to enjoy a meal in such a setting. But when one has to cook in the most primitive fashion and the heat is making one ill and the rations are mildewed, it is really a doubtful pleasure. I have decided to give it up and shall try to confine myself to bread and tea.

Prison tea has to be seen to be believed! My experience of tea is fairly varied, ranging from the exquisitely perfumed and delicate varieties that Madam Chiang sends me to the nondescript syrupy stuff one is obliged to swallow during election campaigns—but never have I seen or tasted anything like jail tea. I am convinced it is some special and very deadly variety of leaf grown for the poor unfortunates who are in prison. Not having any tea of my own I took this decoction once and nearly passed out. It would give me a tremendous thrill if I could make all jail officials live for one week on jail rations. We should not have quite so much talk about the 'well-balanced and wholesome diet'. I wonder why we are always able to plan well-balanced diets for others, but for ourselves we generally try to get the most tasty, forgetting the balance part entirely.

I am going to read a fascinating book Indu has lent me—an anthology of 'The World's Great Letters'. I am looking forward to an interesting evening. I like to keep myself occupied at this hour because, above all others it is the hour when I grow reminiscent and a little homesick. I have no idea how long this term of imprisonment is going to last. I had better shake off such weakness and settle down!

16th August 1942

The first thing I learnt this morning was that there had been firing in the city twice yesterday. The information is not from a source I consider reliable, but nevertheless it has disturbed me. It is terrible to be shut up here when others are exposed to daily dangers.

I was interrupted by the matron who seemed to be in a mood for a chat. Having nothing to say to her I sat silent while she told me the story of her life. There was also a running commentary on the various Superintendents under whom she had served and the Inspector Generals of Prisons she had seen and spoken to. It is amusing to compare notes about jail administration as seen by different matrons. Some day I shall write a book about 'Jails and Matrons I Have Known'. It should make amusing reading. If my term of imprisonment is long enough I should be well acquainted with prison politics—though I seem to have more than a passing knowledge of them already. They are not intricate to anyone who tries to understand a little the workings of the human mind.

I spent an hour last night reading 'The Letters'. Some of them are really beautiful. 'Letters are always interesting—specially if they are other people's,' Voltaire has said. 'The post is the consolation of life,' and some one else has added, 'As long as there are postmen life will have zest.' There must be very few people who have not at some period of their lives recognized the truth of the above sayings. Most of us have waited in breathless suspense for the post which was to bring the one letter we wanted most—maybe it was news of a child far away from us—a friend from whom we have been parted—money on which many things depended—or just a love letter—one of those silly epistles which all lovers write, full of the pleasant nothings which the beloved waits for with so much eagerness and which she imagines are hers alone—forgetting that the same words and sentiments have been shared by all lovers since the beginning of time.

Today the matron has permitted one of the convict girls to come over and help me with my cleaning and cooking etc. Her name is Durgi and she belongs to the potter class. From her history-ticket I see she is twenty-six years old and is serving a sentence for the murder of her husband. She has already done eight years. She is very dark but has good features and pleasing manners. Like all other convicts she wears a pair of tiny drawers and an upper garment which has no special name. The regular jail uniform—skirt and bodice—is too heavy and hot for use in the summer and is only worn on inspection days. Durgi has nice limbs and they are seen to good advantage in her abbreviated costume. I think she and I will be good friends.

There has been a hard shower of rain today and it is cooler at last. The sky is dark with clouds so there will be more rain tonight. The barrack is leaking so badly that there is no spot where my bed can entirely escape. I have chosen a place where my head is safe but where my feet will get a bath! The insects have increased and it is almost impossible to keep the light on—but I do not intend to be beaten so easily. It is only 7.30 p.m. and I cannot possibly go to bed yet—so I shall seek forgetfulness in my book and read Heloise's beautiful letters to Abelard.

There are as rigid social conventions in prison as outside. The woman who is in for abduction is on the lowest rank of the social ladder, then come the counterfeiters of coins, thieves and finally the women who are serving a sentence for murder. These are the leaders and they are tremendously proud of their position. It is usual when a quarrel takes place for a woman to say—'Don't dare to treat me as if I were a common thief—won't stand for it—I am in for murder.' During my first term of imprisonment in 1932 I was a little afraid of this type in the beginning. But soon one recognized how after all any one of us might commit an act of violence in a moment of anger or through sheer force of temper—it wouldn't necessarily degrade us to the level of the human being who commits daily in cold blood acts such as theft, abduction and the like.

17th August 1942

It has rained in torrents since last night. My barrack looks like a lake and the bed an island—the only spot where one can have a degree of safety from the elements. Yet somehow the weather has helped me. It is in keeping with my mood and I do not mind it. I think if the sun had been shining today I would have felt more depressed.

The day has dragged on and I have felt no inclination to do anything—I asked Durgi to make me something to eat thinking in my ignorance that it would be a fairly simple thing for her to do. The dish she presented to me looked like dirty porridge and tasted worse.

Charcoal is not supplied as on previous occasions and the smoke from the damp wood makes cooking very difficult. The rations are of the poorest quality and mixed with grit and dirt, tiny stones and even an odd spider or two thrown in for good weight. After cleaning the dal and rice one finds that the quantity has appreciably diminished. I am keeping the dirt I have taken out of my rations until inspection day and will show it to the doctor. The ghee supplied is dark brown in colour and has a funny smell. There is so little of it, it seems useless to bother about the quality.

Lack of news is irritating. Rumours, of course, come in—a jail is a sort of whispering gallery and the whispers have a habit of echoing and re-echoing round the place, one can't help hearing them, but rumours are not enough and one craves for some real authentic news especially at a time like this. I find myself fretting and losing my temper quite unnecessarily.

18th August 1942

Monday and parade day. The usual hustle and bustle since dawn—shouting, abuse, much running about—and finally, the visit of the Superintendent. It was very brief, thank goodness! I was in no mood for his small talk. He had sent me his cane with a leather flap at the end to use as a fly swat and enquired if it were of any use...'It helps me to relieve my feelings,' I told him, 'even if I do not succeed in killing many flies!'

'Are you satisfied?' he asked. I think what he actually meant was: 'Are you comfortable?'

'Would I be in jail if I were?' I answered. That ended the visit.

The Superintendent's remark gives me food for thought—satisfaction, comfort, happiness, freedom—how meaningless these words have become. I am inclined to agree with Bernard Shaw when he says: 'Only on paper has humanity yet achieved glory, beauty, truth, knowledge, virtue and abiding love.' But that is cynical and it is not right for people like us, engaged in the struggle for freedom, to adopt such a philosophy even in our moments of depression...I must guard against it.

I had just finished the last sentence when a noise at the gate announced another visitor. This time it was the Commissioner who had come. He came straight to my barrack and with a clearing of the throat enquired if I were comfortable. There seemed no point in giving the obvious reply and I don't think he expected one, so I said nothing but just smiled. He looked hurriedly round the barrack and made an orderly retreat.

Today is my birthday and the children sent me a parcel of books—but the pleasure of the gift was short-lived. The Superintendent told me that a new set of regulations had been received and would apply to us. We are to be called 'two' prisoners and shall be placed in the second class ... We shall not be permitted newspapers, letters or interviews or any article from home. Jail clothes will be provided—lock-up will take place. Our allowance will be reduced from 12/- to 9/- per day.

None of these things moved me except the restriction on correspondence. 'How will your children manage without you,' the Superintendent asked me. I said, 'They know how to look after themselves.' He was rather surprised at my answer but agreed and said, 'Yes, they are exceedingly plucky youngsters . . .'

The sad news that Mahadev Desai had died of heart failure in jail on the 15th has come as a great shock and has deeply hurt me. My mind is full of pictures of him. He was a fine person—one of God's good men. We are the poorer for his loss. I wonder where poor Durga and the boy are. Now that Bapu is in prison they have no home. I wish I could send a word of comfort to Durga. Ever since I heard of

Mahadevbhai's death I have been terribly upset. Last night I lay awake and so many incidents connected with him passed through my mind. It seems only the other day that he came to me in Anand Bhawan and asked me to read an article in the *Modern Review* written by a 'dear friend' of his—a young man whom he described as 'most brilliant and very lovable'. The year was 1920, the article was entitled 'At the feet of the Guru' and the name of the author was Ranjit Pandit. For twenty-two years now I have been the wife of this 'most brilliant and very lovable' man. Ranjit and Mahadev were at college together and graduated in the same year. Although they seldom corresponded, there was a deep bond of sympathy and affection between them. The news of Mahadev's passing will hurt Ranjit.

19th August 1942

The common idea about prison seems to be that it is a place where one is exceedingly lonely. Lonely one does feel as in the wrong kind of crowd, but not alone. In no other place have I longed so much for solitude as I have done since coming here a week ago. From dawn to dark there is hardly a moment when I am by myself. Everybody is interested in me, everybody wants to pour out her tale of woe in the hope that I can help her to get out of this place. The noise, complaints about each other, quarrels and free fights—to say nothing of the abuse which is hurled back and forth, is very wearing to the nerves. Even the night is full of sounds—not little, unexpected noises such as one hears outside, but the harsh monotonous constantly repeated noises that jar on the nerves. As Ernst Toller has said about jail in one of his letters: 'Day after day chains of sound are strangling you with their dissonance.' Only those who have been prisoners can understand fully what this means. Of course the noises and lack of privacy seem worse in the beginning; as time goes on one is able, by an effort of will, to keep all the noises away. I have been able to isolate myself completely from a whole barrack full of talking, quarrelling women and carry on the thread of my book as if I was alone. But this takes time and there must be a certain amount of mental calm which, at present, I do not possess.

This place assumes gigantic proportions at night—the tiny flickering light of my jail lantern casts long and weird shadows which have a ghostly appearance. I sit and look at them and weave stories to amuse myself.

The barrack in which I live is a rectangular room intended to accommodate twelve or more convicts. There are gratings at short distances all along each side, one of them being a door which is bolted and locked up at night. One side of the barrack is raised four steps from the ground and serves as a latrine after lock-up. For day use a small bathroom and latrine have been added on to the barrack. This was made for me during my last imprisonment and is certainly a very great help. The whole place is in a state of acute disrepair and the tiles on the roof are in need of renewal. I have only been supplied with a moonj jail cot and a small ricketty iron table. I keep my bed at the furthest end of the barrack from the latrine—previous experience has taught me to bag whatever I can before other prisoners start arriving! My bed is alongside a grating looking into the yard and from which I can see the outer gate. Occasionally, if the wardress who opens it is slow, I can get a glimpse of green grass and a bit of the road. It is surprising how refreshing this glimpse is. We are surrounded by high walls which shut out even the trees. The yard itself is the most dreary place imaginable—there is only one small tree—if I stay here long enough I suppose I shall make some attempt at a garden.

My yard contains one other barrack which is empty at present. There is another yard separated from mine where the convicts live. There are about forty-four women only, as this is a very small jail. They are all habituals and some of them are old acquaintances having been here during my last imprisonment. They are not permitted to come into my yard unless something special has to be done. But when the door between the two yards is open, we exchange greetings and they give me friendly smiles and ask an occasional question about the children, of whom they have heard from me on previous occasions. In the other yard also are the solitary cells. The sight of these always upsets me—they are unfit for any human being to be locked up in. There is a woman there now—I have not been able to find out her offence but I can hear her wailing at intervals throughout the day and night. It is a horrible sound—the wail of a prisoner who has lost all hope and is afraid.

Durgi has been telling me the story of her life. It is a common one—she killed her husband because he neglected her, thrashed her and did not give her enough to eat. She gives me gruesome details of the murder and appears to get a lot of satisfaction from the recital. I try to analyze her feelings later and come to the conclusion that the main cause for her satisfaction is the fact that by killing the husband she has been able to strike a blow at the mother-in-law whom she still hates. She left a little boy of two years at home and came to prison with a baby girl of six weeks who has recently died. Durgi is passionately fond of children and is very cut up at the loss of the child whose death she attributes to black magic. Nothing I can say to the contrary will convince her. She sometimes cries for her son who is now nearly eleven years old and whom she has never seen since her imprisonment.

The number of frogs in this yard is unbelievable. They are all over the place—great big ugly creatures and incredibly foolish looking. They remind me of war profiteers—those smug people who are so content with the little circle in which they move that they completely forget there is a world outside it. In the evening when the frogs begin to croak I get quite exhausted. Sometimes there is a solitary croak and at other times a regular chorus which increases in volume and drives one crazy. Yesterday I stepped out of bed hurriedly and without looking down put my foot on a big toad! It was rather awful—but he survived and hopped out into the yard.

The tiny kitten which used to occupy my cell in 1941 has grown into a big and very ugly cat. She comes and steals any food that happens to be lying around and as she is more than half-starved it is impossible to shoo her away. I find it hard to be kind to her as I am a little allergic to cats and not quite at my ease in their company. So far no mice and rats have invaded this barrack but I have no doubt they will come. In 1941, my life was one long misery owing to a family of rats who had the complete run of this place.

While the door between the two yards was open I had a brief glimpse of several familiar faces. Sharbati is still here, looking thinner and more ill than when I saw her last. She tells me she still suffers from her old complaint and has been coughing up blood. Naraini is here too and like Johnnie Walker she is still going strong. I hear she threatened to commit suicide one day last year by climbing on to the *neem* tree in the yard, and tying a corner of her sheet round her neck and another corner to a branch of the tree. There was a terrific commotion. The other convicts implored her not to give up her life, she insisted that unless her sentence was reduced she would kill herself. Entreaties and threats of the matron proving equally futile, the Superintendent was sent for. I do not know what magic he used but he persuaded her to come down. Theatrical to the end, she jumped down and broke a rib and fractured her arm. She showed me the marks on her arm with great pride.

I am a little afraid of Naraini. This is her eleventh conviction and she is in for seven years for having stolen a sheet. She looks most unwomanly and being very dark with close cropped hair and several broken teeth she is not pleasing to the sight. She has a supple body and can climb trees with the speed and agility of a cat in spite of being nearly fifty. She refuses to burden herself with clothes and wears the bare minimum. She has a passion for colour and talks with feeling about the colourful clothes she has possessed in the past. So long as she is left to herself, she behaves, but if she is roused she becomes almost inhuman in her fury. She can use abusive language with deadly effect and her tempers generally end in a storm of tears.

I see other faces that I know but I cannot remember the names. I suppose they will come back to me later.

The wardresses here are a strange collection. There are five of them—Zohra, Zainab, Vishnudei, Shyama and Mrs Solomon.

Zohra is a deadly female. Incredibly dirty in her person and in her habits, she is a born cringer and looks unreliable. I feel we are not going to be friends. Zainab is a fat, placid woman very talkative and full of anecdotes of her past. Service in a prison has not warped her and her sense of humour is quite delicious. Vishnudei is tall and strapping. In size and physique she is the ideal wardress and looks imposing in her uniform. She is reticent and does not speak much. Shyama is a negative person altogether, the type one hardly ever notices. Mrs Solomon seems the nicest of the lot—as a human being she is superior to the rest and is gentle in manner. A Christian, she looks upon herself as being in a different class to the others and, in the way of Christian converts in India, her standard has been raised beyond her status in life and she is in constant financial difficulties. Already I know her domestic troubles—there are so many that the poor dear has to seek relief in speaking about them. She has a fine face, soft eyes and grey hair. It is a pity she is connected with a jail.

20th August 1942

This morning I woke up early before unlocking and lay looking up at our roof. The barrack is even more dilapidated than before. The ceiling falls in chunks every day and makes a mess all over my bed and on the floor. The tiles are badly placed and sun and rain come in as they please. These days the glare gets very strong and I have to keep on my sunglasses most of the day. The floor is so uneven that one cannot walk across the barrack at night without stumbling. The bats and frogs are frequent visitors and I live in terror of them.

I am writing this after midnight as it seems to be the only quiet period. Today was specially noisy but the night is calm and peaceful in spite of the counting of the prisoners which we can hear at intervals all night.

I sit at my grating and watch the stars twinkle. They give one a feeling of security. They are always the same, serene and undisturbed and the follies of men do not worry them. Sometimes a moonbeam also steals in and lies across the floor like a silver stream. Occasionally I hear planes fly overhead—the sound makes me feel restless. I want to break through my bars and fly. It is absurd to keep human beings locked up in this fashion—it solves no problem and creates new difficulties. The world moves in a circle and we always come back to the starting point. Progress is only a word; what does it mean I wonder!

There has been a terrific commotion again today. One of the convicts was due to have an interview with a relative. The poor man had come a very long distance and spent money that he could ill afford. On arrival a wardress told him he could not have an interview unless she was paid. This is the usual thing and as a rule relatives of prisoners are aware of it. The man first begged to be excused as he was poor but finally produced two rupees which were pocketed. When the woman was taken out the wardress found some petty fault and started a quarrel with her and she was ordered back to her cell and the interview cancelled. Of course we all knew the reason. The poor woman howled all day and her friends hurled abuse at the jail authorities.

The amount of bribery that goes on is shocking. It is done in all sorts of ways, sometimes quite openly. Says Geffray Mynshul: 'A prison is a grave to bury men alive, a place wherein a man for half a year's imprisonment may learn more law than he can at Westminster for a hundred pounds. It is a microcosmos, a little world of woe, it is a map of misery, it is a place that will learn a young man more villainy if he be apt to take it in one half year, than he can learn at twenty bowling allies, brothel houses or ordinaries; and an old man more policy than if he had been a pupil to Machiavelli. It is a place that hath more diseases predominant in it than the pest house in plague time and it stinks more than the Lord Mayor's doghouse in August.'

21st August 1942

Last night I could not sleep. I walked up and down the barrack. Then I read for sometime but beyond the fact that my eyes were tired, sleep still remained as far away as ever. I lay down with my eyes closed hoping to doze off but no such luck—twelve—one—two—three—I tossed from side to side and counted the hours. Finally, soon after three I fell asleep and dreamt a strange dream, inspired no doubt by my thoughts about prison life on the previous evening.

I was in a solitary cell. It was hardly high enough for me to stand up in and by stretching my arms I could touch the walls on either side. The roof leaked and the rain fell in huge drops on my head and as the raindrops touched me they became rupees and hurt my head and I cried to get out. But the cell was locked, and there was no escape. The silver raindrops continued to fall and they bored a hole in my head. The pain was so bad I felt I must die, then suddenly I woke up! I was in bed in my barrack—the rain was pouring outside. From the leaking roof, big drops were falling on my forehead and above the noise of the rain came the voices of the wardresses on duty shouting at some unfortunate prisoner in the next yard.

After this dream it was not possible to get back to sleep and so I lay and watched the light grow, and presently the bugle sounded and it was time for unlocking. But I stayed in bed feeling tired and disinclined to face the day and as I lay a rhyme, read somewhere long ago, came to my mind—

As he went through cold Bath Fields
he saw a solitary cell
And the Devil was pleased, for it
gave him a hint
For improving the prisons in Hell.

I do not of course know what the prisons in hell are like but if I finally get as far as the nether regions, I shall be able to give the Devil quite a few hints on their improvement after my growing experience of prisons in British India. I might also be able to recommend to him some really efficient jailors, matrons, wardresses and the like. After all they will be wanting jobs, and what so good as work with which they are already acquainted.

The first thing I did this morning was to go and look at the little room adjoining the other barrack which I had converted into a nursery last year for the babies of the convicts. I found that it had been turned into half-storeroom, half-office—the friezes painted on the walls had almost faded out—the clay toys I had especially modelled were broken and lying in bits on a shelf, the straw mats on which the children sat had disappeared, and the blackboard was broken and lay covered with dust in a corner.

All this was sad enough but what proved much worse was the condition of the children themselves. Some of them have gone as their mothers have been released but a few of the old batch remain. They are again running wild, and are completely neglected. The few things we had succeeded in teaching them last year are forgotten and all the evil habits seem to have returned. I found Jamni chewing tobacco. Her mother (who has been out once during the last few months and came back for theft) tells me she cannot do without it. Munshi does not seem to have grown a single inch in these last fifteen months. His front teeth are decayed and he is much thinner and lacking in energy. Only his beautiful eyes remain the same. It is difficult to believe he is seven years old.

There is one new baby, an adorable infant called 'Shakko'. She is two and half years old, has grey eyes and a lovely golden complexion and honey-coloured hair. Her mother is a habitual and is in for theft—her seventh conviction—a horrible witch-like creature. I cannot imagine how she produced anything as perfect as Shakko. Besides these three little ones there is one other child who does not seem quite normal.

I have also discovered that the convicts are not having their regular lessons in Hindi and Urdu this year. The teacher—Mrs Bothaju—spends the morning conducting a class for children of the warders in their quarters. Any children belonging to the women convicts go out and join this class. In the afternoon Mrs Bothaju is supposed to teach the women but so far I have seen no signs of it. The girls hate learning and the teacher is only too glad to have a siesta. On inspection days books and slates are always within sight but it does not seem to strike the inspecting officials that they might put a few questions and discover for themselves whether there is any improvement.

22nd August 1942

This afternoon at 2 o'clock it suddenly began to rain in torrents—in a few minutes the barrack had begun to leak and the next half-hour was spent in dragging the bed about to a place of safety. The rain beat through the bars and fell in great big drops from the roof. Eventually I lay down and let the foot of the bed get wet, curling up my feet to protect them. The rain stopped as suddenly as it began and now the sky is clear and blue and the atmosphere very muggy.

All my clothes and the few articles of food are getting mildewed. Everything smells horribly including the clothes I am wearing. I wonder what it will be like when the jail clothes are provided. It is just as well that we are used to wearing khadi!

I am worried about my books. The new rule by which books and periodicals come through the District Magistrate means that half the books will never reach us and those that do get here will take many weeks to accomplish the journey. I have a perfect horror of being left without anything to read. The days are so incredibly long and the prison nights surely contain more hours than any others. Time lengthens out, 'each day a month, each month a year' until one has lived through a century. The Superintendent asked me on my birthday how old I was. 'I do not know,' I said, 'I feel as if I had lived through centuries.' Later I was reminded of a quotation: 'No hourglass, no diary can estimate for you the fullness of time; it is the soul that fills it; if the soul lie asleep, it is not filled at all; if it be awake, in the vigils of suspense, of sorrow, of aspiration, there may be more in an hour than you can find in a dozen empty lives. It is not larger time that we want, so much as the more capacious soul to flow through every pore of the little which we have.' I suppose it is 'the more capacious soul' that is at the present moment, making me feel as if I had lived through centuries!

There have been more than the usual quarrels today and even now when lock-up has taken place there is no peace. The beauty of the night is being made hideous with harsh sounds. In the evenings I like to sit near my grating and watch the drifting clouds pass in the sky and wait for the stars to come out. It is fascinating to watch them twinkle. So far there has been no moon but I am looking forward to her visits later on. She is not a lady to be relied on, being a coquette, she is full of moods. Jails do not please her, but sometimes I watch her playing hide and seek with the clouds and she sends a silver beam into the barrack by way of greeting and to show that she still remembers me.

23rd August 1942

I couldn't sleep again last night and was tired when I got up this morning. To make matters worse I had various aches and pains and a fit of depression all at the same time. I was idle the whole morning not being in the mood to read or write or do anything else. Owing to the rain I couldn't go into the yard and kept walking inside for over an hour feeling caged and restless. Finally I lay down. In the afternoon matron came in with four books sent by a friend. 'Oh the little more, how much it is!' My depression vanished in a moment. Someone had thought of me and this little contact with the outside world made things more easy. The books look interesting and I am no longer afraid of the evening.

24th August 1942

Prison also has its humours—'Do you know,' said matron to me yesterday, 'when I unlock your barrack each morning I try not to disturb you because I know you do not sleep well at night. But I was thinking I should by rights call out to you because, if you were to die in the night, how should I know ...' She is, I suppose, what one would call a 'Job's comforter.' Happy thought that I should die in the night, yet I expect there are worse deaths!

I have read one of the books that the girls sent

me for my birthday: 'Escape from Freedom'. It is charmingly written and holds one's interest. I am keeping the book of plays for one of my dark days. God forbid that they should come too soon! I've had my share of dark days for a bit and they are just beginning to turn faintly grey—-but I'm hoping that soon they will be all rose-coloured. Fortunately, I was born an optimist.

Last evening about four, another woman political prisoner was brought in. She turns out to be the wife of R.N.S. Her husband and father-in-law are already in jail and although she has done no political work at all she has been arrested. She has a small child of seven years—a girl—and no one to leave her with and is very unhappy. Later on there was more excitement and who should come in but Purnima! I was glad to see her and we talked far into the night. Afterwards I lay awake until the early hours. The yard was flooded with moonlight and looked almost beautiful. But even beauty makes one restless in prison.

Today was Parade day again with the usual fuss. Mr Gardener told us that Urmila Tripathi had not come as one of us ('two' prisoner) but had been arrested for arson and looting and would probably have to be treated as an ordinary convict. This is absurd as the girl is quite incapable of doing anything that requires energy or agility. She is a dull, placid person with no interest in anything but her home and whose knowledge of politics is nil.

It has been a terribly hot day and the sun shines straight into the barrack all the afternoon.

25th August 1942

Last night was very sultry and hot, but the yard was bathed in silver light all night.

It is still hot and very muggy this morning and we seem to be in for a bad day. My head has ached ever since I got up and the throbbing is increasing in spite of the Aspro that I have taken. It is not going to be a very cheerful day for me, I'm afraid!

26th August 1942

Purnima has brought a calendar with her. At first I was glad to see it but now I find that it has a disturbing effect on the mind. What is the use of a calendar unless one has something to look forward to—some day standing out from amongst the rest? For us it is better not to see dates and count days.

Last evening, just before lock-up, another woman—Janki Devi—was brought in on a charge of arson and looting at a small wayside station in this district. She was straightway bustled out of our yard and into one of the solitary confinement cells. On asking the matron why she had been treated in this fashion we were told that this was done according to police instructions. We argued about this and asked matron to look up the jail manual and also consult the Superintendent. There was no reason at all why two women arrested for the same offence should be treated differently. Finally matron came back about an hour after lock-up and transferred Janki Devi to the barrack in which Urmila Tripathi has been kept. This was a great relief to Purnima and me.

This morning I have seen and talked to Janki Devi. She is a widow and she was studying at the Normal School in Allahabad. She seems a fairly intelligent person.

The heat continues and the barrack is like an oven. The perspiration pours down my face and body in a constant stream and my head aches. I am ashamed of myself and these constant aches and pains. On former occasions I was always able to adjust myself to jail routine within a day or two and was able to occupy every moment of my time. There were fits of depression sometimes and once in a while the thought of the children made me feel restless—but the present feeling is quite different. I cannot settle down to anything at all and looking across the room I find Purnima in a similar condition! Well I suppose we shall adjust ourselves in time.

I am told today is Raksha-Bandhan. This morning Mrs Bothaju, the prison-teacher arrived with a bright yellow rakhi tied round her wrist, contrasting beautifully with the ebony of her skin. It was the only sign we had in jail of this beautiful festival.

It has rained at last in torrents and the heat has subsided for the moment.

27th August 1942

'Give me the strength to raise my mind above daily trifles.'

Another day, but so like the last and all the ones

that have gone before that it might be the same. One feels numb as if the power to feel or think had gone. 'My head aches and a drowsy numbness fills my brain ...'

Zainab brought some gay-coloured rakhis for the matron today. She was born a Hindu, but when quite young was abducted from her husband's home, converted to Islam and married. She has stuck to this man all these years and works in order to keep him in comfort. She observes the Hindu festivals, and even bathes in the Ganges. She is polite and quarrels less than the rest and is generally good-humoured and placid. In fact her placidity has made her spread and spread until she looks in the distance, like a large ball made out of odd bits of bright coloured rags and her walk is the satisfied waddle of an old duck.

Our imprisonment is a constant source of worry to her and she offers up frequent prayers for the welfare of my family. My meals are another of her worries—she tries to persuade me to eat what she calls 'proper food'. It distresses her to see anyone eat bread and butter and drink so much tea. When I draw her attention to her own large proportions and say I have no desire to spread like her, she raises her eyes to heaven and says, 'That has nothing to do with food—it is kismet.' At present she is disturbed at the thought of a possible Japanese invasion as she feels she will not be able to run away, owing to her bulk and she has heard the Japs are cannibals! Horrible thought!

28th August 1942

Another very hot, stifling day—the barrack is full of flies, gnats, ants and all manner of insects. The perspiration flows off our faces and bodies and keeps us in a sort of miniature Turkish bath. There is thunder in the air but no rains so far.

Lekha sent some copies of *Life* and *Time* the other day. They have helped me to pass several dull hours and the advertisements are a source of constant interest. They make me think of Ritu!

I have had no news of Ranjit since he left for Bombay three weeks ago and am beginning to worry about him. I wish I could communicate with him to tell him to be careful about his health. Not knowing Bhai's whereabouts is also worrying me. I hope he is well and does not want for anything.

The heat makes it impossible to do anything

except lie on one's bed and gasp. From where I lie I look through my grating to the gate in the yard and weave a chain of stories round the small iron door in the gate. 'The Tragedy of The Closed Door' would sound well.

The matron is going out again this evening and comes in all dressed up in a pale pink creation, which, she tells me, she had made especially for the farewell party given to the last Superintendent! Why do all matrons dye their hair? That is a problem that has been worrying me for a long time! I think one of these days I shall let myself go and dye my own hair a bright red. It will be a form of release!

29th August 1942

Last night the heat continued to be stifling and the barrack seemed to be closing in and suffocating us. The mosquitoes filled the place in ever increasing swarms and the noise of their humming in the stillness of the night was an intolerable sound. All night long we turned and tossed and just as it was beginning to get somewhat bearable about 4.30 a.m. the bugle sounded and then goodbye to all hopes of sleep.

From the moment the barracks are unlocked, the volume of sound goes on increasing until, after an hour or so, it reaches such a pitch that one cannot hear oneself think. It is, of course, quite impossible to lie in bed under such conditions, however tired one may feel. Then gradually things begin to settle down and by about 8 o'clock there is a certain amount of quiet in the prison yard. By that time it is too late to go back to bed—and one looks forward to a quiet afternoon nap. But as the afternoon approaches the flies increase, the glare and heat make one feel dizzy and millions of tiny black gnats swarm all over the place ready to annoy and disturb one. It is too hot to cover one's face, and to keep it exposed means attacks from flies and gnats—so one lies in bed, fans away the flies and tries to keep cool. Then the fan slips out of the hand as sleep overpowers one for a few minutes until the flies, grown more bold, start running races over one's face, and with a start one is awake again and the fan is hastily brought into operation!

30th August 1942

This morning I woke up feeling very tired and ill.

There was no inclination to leave my bed, but owing to the noise and the dust raised by the sweeping of the yard I was obliged to get up. About 9 o'clock I had some tea and had just settled down to read when an exclamation from Purnima drew my attention to the grating. What was my surprise to see Lekha, laden with flower garlands striding into the yard behind the matron!

I couldn't understand what had brought her here. First the idea flashed through my mind that she had come to interview me—but why the flowers? Then, for one fleeting instant, perhaps we are being released. By this time Lekha was inside the barrack and was announcing in triumphant tones that she had been arrested. It came as an almost unbelievable blow. Lekha arrested! Why surely Lekha was only a baby still—not nearly old enough to understand politics, let alone live them.

As I stood listening to her telling Purnima excitedly, how the arrest took place, I was quite unable to speak, and kept seeing pictures of her right through these eighteen years.

First as a chubby baby lying on the Juhu sand, then learning to walk and talk. Lekha at her first Montessori school. That terrible period of her illness and her almost miraculous recovery—a rebirth in more senses than one. Lekha at the railway station on her way to school in Poona just before Ranjit and I were arrested in 1932—she sat silent and wide-eyed, a solemn little person of eight, blinking away the tears and clutching a big tricolour flag. 'Don't carry that big flag darling,' I had said, and she replied, 'It's to frighten the police away with!'

Then another: a picture of her gay in a Fair Isle sweater and smart Jodhpurs just back from her lesson at the riding school at Rajkot, bright-eyed and excited, 'Oh Mum!—The master says I may learn to jump Cocktail soon—won't that be fun?' Lekha in the swimming pool. And gradually a bigger Lekha, still simple but full of *joie de vivre*—and with a new understanding of life—Lekha at her eighteenth birthday party—so happy, extracting the utmost out of every minute. And, the last picture of this group, Lekha as she stood saying goodbye to me on the steps at Anand Bhawan on the night of my arrest. Again a new Lekha with a new purpose in her eyes—more determined, a dependable young person.

And here she is in prison—what a coming of age! For her, perhaps, this was inevitable.

The thought of Tara and Rita in Anand Bhawan alone; the house surrounded by police and C.I.D. men, is tormenting me.

The story of the arrest is the usual comic opera affair—police, armed guards, C.I.D. men and the usual paraphernalia went to Anand Bhawan about 9 p.m. yesterday. The girls had gone out with friends to a picnic at Ram Bagh. The Inspector asked for Lekha and was informed that she was out. They waited and meanwhile produced a warrant for the search of her room. When this was over and nothing incriminating found, Lekha was still not back so they went away. This morning the arrest took place at 8 o'clock. Lekha informs us that although she was seething with excitement, she was determined to appear casual and actually ate an extra piece of toast for breakfast just to make the police wait and show them that she regarded this event as of no special importance! Obviously an attempt to imitate Mamaji (Jawaharlal Nehru).

31st August 1942

Lekha has brought the news that Tangle (the children's cairn terrier) is suffering terribly. At my request the Superintendent sent a message to the house that the poor little mite should be put out of his misery if there was no chance of a cure. All night I was sorely troubled by visions of the 'wee one' suffering and no one near him.

Heard from the Superintendent that he had telephoned the house again and got in touch with Tara. The vet has been and has given Tangle some medicine which has soothed him. He is doing his best and is hoping to save him.

Lekha has developed a cold. I hope it will not grow. Jail is not a good place to be indisposed in.

We have heard with some excitement that Bijjubhabi (Mrs Rameshwari Nehru) has been arrested in Lahore!

1st September 1942

From today our clocks have been advanced by one hour. This will affect us adversely because lock-up takes place at 6 p.m. as usual, only now it will actually be 5 o'clock and we shall lose one hour of freedom—the best hour too in the cool of the evening.

Last night the air was delightful and the mosquitoes left us in peace. It was the first restful night we have had for sometime.

The gratings between our yard and the one in which the ordinary convicts live have been closed up. We are dangerous people and cannot be permitted to corrupt the innocent minds of the habitual convicts.

Lekha and I read Bernard Shaw together and enjoyed him. There has been some rain and it is fresh and cool. Having finished Shaw's play we read a modern comedy, 'Drawing Room', by Thomas Browne after lock-up. It describes a family not unlike our own and we had a good many laughs over it.

2nd September 1942

A cool night. Rain this morning, but it was only a passing shower and now it looks as if the weather is likely to be sultry during the day.

Tangle is no more. The news has just come that he was put out of his suffering last night by an injection. Poor little loved one!

4th September 1942

The ways of Providence and prison officials are inscrutable. We are allowed nine annas a day for our food—for the first week I was here, before these new rules came into force, the allowance was twelve annas. My daily rations never exceeded seven annas. I asked if the balance could be kept to my credit and fruit supplied to me once a week. 'Oh yes,' said the jail and I thought 'how very obliging!' Little did I know! The fruit came the first week, such as it was, and since then eternal chits and messages, all to no effect. The money due to us accumulates and the fruit does not arrive and thus we learn a valuable lesson in patience!

I seem to have been on the warpath ever since I came here. I have not worried the prison authorities so much on former occasions—but this time things are intolerable. If I order fruit, it takes, from ten to twelve days to arrive and finally six bananas, well squashed, are handed to me. Naturally I return them immediately. Next morning a chit from the office: 'Who is to pay for the bananas?' 'Of course the jail,' I reply. More chits from the office, more requests for fruit from me—meanwhile the balance of my daily nine annas is accumulating. When I point out that no fruit has arrived and nearly two rupees are due to me, I am told the contractor cannot find any fruit in the market!

In sheer despair I write to the Superintendent and say that if the contractor is a dishonest rogue there is no earthly reason why I should be his victim. If my fruit does not come I shall make a formal complaint to a higher authority. Result, a flutter in the jail dovecotes and two lovely Kashmir apples! The price too is lovely! Actually I don't care if I have fruit or not, or in fact, anything at all—but there is no reason why the jail should benefit because I happen to eat less than my daily allowance.

5th September 1942

I got up in a terrific temper this morning. It rained all last evening in torrents and most of the night. The barrack is full of water and there is hardly enough room to sit down in a dry spot. During the night, part of my bed got wet through and Lekha was soaked. It is dark and dismal and everything jars on the nerves. The wood is so wet that we cannot light a fire—there is no milk although it is 9 o'clock. I suppose there will be no rations either until it clears up. If one rainy day can upset the organization of a central prison in this way, I shudder to think what would happen in the event of an enemy invasion! It is easy to imagine what must have happened in Burma when the convicts and lunatics were hurriedly released from their respective prisons.

Purnima is making desperate efforts to light a stove with some coal saved from the kitchen. She and Bhagawandei—the lumbardarni—are fanning for all they are worth, but so far the only result is the smoke which is filling up the barrack. No sign of a fire yet.

The milk arrived at 9.20 a.m.! Still no rations. Eventually things began to turn up in bits and had all arrived by afternoon. There has been a great deal of excitement because the matron has the weekend off.

6th September 1942

We had a heavy downpour all night long but it stopped towards morning and is now clearing up. The milk is always delayed now and comes between nine and ten and we cool our heels until it arrives, the rations come at about 10.30, the vegetables at eleven—the bread about four, and if we are lucky, the evening ration of milk comes along just as we are being locked up.

Everything is so delightfully vague in jail—nobody is responsible for anything—the right way of doing things is always abandoned in favour of the wrong one and so we go on from day to day.

The rations supplied to us get daily worse. Some articles are so bad that we cannot use them at all. Potatoes are not supplied because the market price is high and the overhead charges of the contractor higher and our allowance is not sufficient to pay for them. There are plenty of vegetables in the jail garden but ours are supplied from the bazar. The jail produce goes first to the high officials, and then filters down gradually to the various underlings, who in turn, share it with their own hangers-on. Naturally, there is none left for the political prisoners.

The cooked food that comes for the convicts is horrible both in appearance and taste. I have often eaten the cooked jail ration, on former occasions and though there has always been much room for improvement, they have never been of such poor quality as the food now supplied. The dal is just dirty water with a handful of red chillies floating on top. The vegetable is always the same and is, I should imagine, cooked without first being washed. One cannot afford to look into it too closely for fear of what may be found inside. The quantity is very small. Rotis are also full of grit.

The food is cooked in the men's section of the prison and sent to our side in large buckets—several portions are removed daily during transit. The result is, some women get less than their share and there is a terrific row every few days.

I am in disgrace with the authorities. Some time ago I asked if I could be given coffee instead of tea in my ration. I was informed that there was no mention of coffee in the jail manual, only tea was mentioned. Government sanction was necessary for this and the Superintendent said he would find out if it could be obtained. After three weeks I was told that I could buy a tin of coffee provided I gave up my tea ration—I ordered half a pound and was charged one rupee and 4 annas by the jail contractor for what costs 14 annas in the market. The daily allowance is 9 annas so I had to pay two days allowance plus two annas more—and as this amount of coffee will only last me a fortnight I shall have to go without rations for two days every fortnight. My health will no doubt improve by a few fasts. In any case, I prefer the coffee to the food, so actually I stand to gain. It is only the absurdity of the jail methods which proves so annoying at times.

7th September 1942

Monday again! Parade day seems to come round with great rapidity, but looking at the calendar one doesn't seem to have advanced very far!

This evening, the matron was walking with me in the yard before lock-up and described the heroism of a young Russian girl who was one of a guerilla band. She was impressed with the way in which she cut telegraph wires and tampered with railway lines and burnt several wayside stations, etc. At the end of the story I could not resist saying, very quietly, 'Those are some of the charges against Janki, only in the language of the foreign government in this country, it is called arson and treason, not heroism. We get a seven-year sentence for it even when sufficient proof is not available.'

Naturally the conversation died after this.

8th September 1942

Last night quantities of the ceiling dropped on me and disturbed my sleep. It meant getting up each time and shaking the bedclothes. About 2.30 a.m. Lekha gave a shout and bounded out of the bed. A large bat had fallen from the roof right on her chest! We got him off the bed but he kept on circling round and round for what seemed hours. Anyway, we were much too frightened to sleep well after that! Who says prison life is lacking in thrills?

10th September 1942

Someone sent us a bunch of zinnias today. It is surprising what a difference a few bright flowers can make even in this drab place.

11th September 1942

Half an hour after lock-up yesterday there was a tremendous knocking at the outer gate and the matron came in excitedly announcing: 'Mrs Indira is here.' A minute later Indu followed by five other women came in! The others are Ram Kali Devi,

Mahadevi Chaube, Lakshmibai Bapat and two young girls: Vidyavati and Govindi Devi. It appears that the women intended to have a meeting but before it could commence the police arrived and made an attempt to arrest Indu and some others who were there. There was a scuffle between the crowd and police. Indu was pulled about and bruised and had her clothes torn. Finally they were brought here. Feroze has also been arrested. There was great excitement in our barrack. Indu was put in here and the others in the barrack opposite. They talked excitedly for a long time after we had composed ourselves.

Indu has no news of Bhai which is very disturbing. Bapu's news, the little she had, was also not good.

Ranjit has been very unwell and could not leave Bombay. He plans to spend ten days in Khali before returning to Allahabad. I am terribly worried about Ranjit. He wants such careful looking after.

12th September 1942

The old Maharastrian lady is going to prove a sore trial to us all. I have known her before in 1932, but fortunately at that time our paths lay in different directions. I was transferred to Lucknow after my trial and she was sent to Fatehgarh. This time it looks as if we shall have to put up with her for the duration! God help us! She chants the Gita by the hour in a loud, raucous voice both morning and evening and for the remainder of the time she tells the world at large the glories of Maharastra and of her ancestors. She is about sixty-odd years old.

13th September 1942

Today has been another hot day, perhaps one of our hottest. I have had three baths all to no effect. I have been able to eat very little for the last two days. It is annoying and I can't go on swallowing medicines every day of the month. Indu is running a temperature. She doesn't look at all well. We have discovered that Vidyavati is pregnant, and that Govindi is only twelve years old! I think both should be released. It is ridiculous to put a young pregnant woman in prison whose only offence is that she attended a meeting—and a child who is still almost a baby. What has this government come to.

There is a new moon this evening. It hangs like a

silver sickle just above the casual barrack and looks delicate and lovely. Indu, Lekha and I have been drawing up a plan—I am to cook the midday meal and they will arrange the supper, in the morning there is nothing very much to be done as we only have tea.

The girls are planning to do a good lot of reading and Indu is going to help Lekha with her French. Lekha has also asked for permission to have her books so that she may continue her studies and prepare for her examination. As we have no chairs or tables it will not be too easy to study. The other day I asked for a chair but was told there were none in the jail storeroom. What we require even more urgently than a chair is a meat-safe in which we can keep our rations. The ants get into the sugar and the cat drinks the milk.

15th September 1942

I have been reading Laurence Housman's autobiography—'The Unexpected Years'. In describing his schooldays he says: 'Defenders of the public school system—as it existed in my days, and as they would like it to continue—maintain that the bullying of small boys is good for them and has a healthy and hardening effect on their characters. It may be so, but what of its effects on those who do the bullying? It seemed to me a cowardly and despicable thing for the strong to afflict the weak; and I am inclined to think that the divine right of Imperialism to swagger through the world, exploiting subject races for their supposed benefit has very largely had its origin in the bullying and fagging which have been countenanced in our public schools.'

And, in another place he says: 'My school experience taught me early the truth of that wise Greek saying, inscribed in the Temple at Delphi: "Would you know a man, give him power." Wherever I have seen power in operation—the kind of power which its admirers are fond of describing as "benevolent despotism" its effect has always been to show very plainly the true character of the man—the good and the bad of him; and very seldom indeed have I found human nature capable of sustaining the burden without moral and intellectual deterioration both in the operator and those on whom he operated. The atavism of cruelty is far too deeply ingrained in the human race for even saints to be entrusted with uncontrolled power over the lives of others…'

This requires no comment!

17th September 1942

I am coming to the conclusion that I am an anti-social creature. The more I see of my fellows, the more my thoughts turn to solitude! During the fortnight I was here by myself I felt lonely sometimes, naturally, and not having adjusted myself to jail life I was also worried about the happenings in the world outside and about the children. But these disturbances would gradually have settled down. I have spent months alone in prison before and never felt the need of companionship.

The last few days have been so noisy that one has hardly had time to hear oneself think. Reading has become impossible and my nerves are frayed to bits. And, as if this wasn't enough, the new orders are that all prisoners should be counted in the usual way every fifteen minutes throughout the night, which means that there will be a harsh medley of sound depriving us of sleep. Truly the ways of jail officials are beyond scrutiny and reason.

19th September 1942

Ranjit was arrested at 6 o'clock this morning at Anand Bhawan. He returned from Bombay the night before last. Poor Tara and Rita! I was hoping they would have at least a week with their father. But these days man proposes and the British Government disposes.

Feroze has been sentenced to one year's rigorous imprisonment and Rs 200/- fine. Personally, I would far rather know the length of my sentence than be suspended as we are in mid-air, so to speak. The length of a sentence either in my own case or in that of others has never bothered me very much.

20th September 1942

This morning quite suddenly the Superintendent said he had no authority to give me coffee. Rules were quoted—the idea being that although rules did not permit, they were trying to accommodate me. I lost my temper completely and said, I wanted no favours. The coffee could go back. I am sorry to say I threw the tin on the ground at the Superintendent's feet! Later I was informed that I could buy coffee instead of tea and there would be no difficulty.

23rd September 1942

Lekha had a very restless night and the boils seem no nearer to bursting than they were yesterday. The pain seems bad and she looks very exhausted. Her temperature persists—between 99 degrees and 100 degrees. Indu was allowed to sleep outside last night—but she had a bad night in spite of it, as her bed was in the veranda and the wind at night comes from the opposite direction. We didn't remember this fact until it was too late for the bed to be moved.

24th September 1942

Last evening I felt suddenly exhausted for no apparent reason. By eight I could hardly sit up and as soon as I had finished bandaging Lekha's arm I lay down and fell into a deep sleep for about forty-five minutes. At night I slept badly although it was cool and there were very few mosquitoes. I felt better today, though still far from bright.

Lekha's boil seems to have extended and the top skin has come off—underneath a small head has appeared, but this has happened before and yet the boil is no nearer bursting. I am tired of it and poor Lekha must be thoroughly fed up, yet she is extraordinarily patient.

Indu had a better night. She slept inside but it was cool and so she slept fairly well.

27th September 1942

Everything as usual. The days are so alike, that time almost seems to stand still. Even Lekha's boil has been affected by the prison atmosphere and seems to have stopped growing! Indu has been much brighter since yesterday—looks better too. Her temperature remains 99.2 degrees morning and evening with an occasional rise of two to four points on the days she is tired or in pain.

28th September 1942

We hear that Feroze has been brought here, along with over a hundred others from Malacca, and has been placed in the C class. This is disturbing news.

We are told that Indu has been recommended for release on grounds of health. Her temperature persists.

I had decided to resume my Monday fasts from today but have been feeling so weak and low since yesterday that I thought it best to wait.

Everybody seems to have a cold. I am surrounded by sneezes and coughs. I wonder how long it will be before I succumb. This barrack freezes in winter and is like an oven in the summer, a really delightful place. Who builds jails?

The night is pitch-dark. I cannot even distinguish the outline of the outer wall which looks much more huge and forbidding at night. It is as if a black velvet curtain had been hung up in order to prevent us from looking into the yard.

More and more political prisoners come into the men's section every day.

We hear the police lorries drawing up outside and then the shouting of slogans by which we know it is our own people who are being brought in. Sometimes we have been able to hear the sound of boys being thrashed on the other side of our yard. By a little judicious questioning we were able to ascertain that such events are not infrequent.

Students are arrested in large batches and many of them thrashed and later on released. Some of these boys are mere children who joined in a procession or attended a meeting.

1st October 1942

It is a lovely crisp morning. I had a better night, and I feel fresher than I have done for some time.

Munshi and little Shakko have been ill for nearly ten days; today after much agitation we persuaded the matron to ask the senior doctor to examine them.

Apparently they have flu and a touch of bronchitis, but nothing has been done. Shakko is very bad and has had no nourishment either. The callous way in which convicts and their children are treated has to be seen to be believed. To be really ill in jail is about the worst punishment I can think of for any human being.

The old Maharastrian lady—Lakshmibai Bapat is back. This time as an undertrial C class prisoner! God help us!

2nd October 1942

Bapu's 74th birthday.

3rd October 1942

The mornings and nights are getting pleasant. Today even at 11 a.m. it is still tolerably cool.

Lekha's boil seems to have gone for good leaving behind a small lump which is being treated with iodine ointment. There is no pain so she is now able to get back more or less to her normal routine of study and exercise.

Two days ago, just before lock-up, a young girl was brought in with a tiny two-month-old baby. She is a C class undertrial prisoner and apparently her only offence is that she was walking along a road with a flag. Her husband was arrested for distributing Congress leaflets ten days ago. She is the vaguest person I have ever seen. Sublimely unconscious of what goes on around her and unable even to look after her baby which, by the way, is her third. I find life inexplicable at times—just one gigantic 'why' to which no reply is forthcoming.

4th October 1942

Yesterday the doctor informed me that Indira, Lekha and I had been placed in A class and that in future we would be entitled to 12 annas per day ration money. Ranjit and Dr Katju had also been so classified. He had no further information so we could not tell on what grounds this classification had been made and what other privileges it implied. In any case, I felt this was wrong and until I knew further details I could not possibly accept the additional money. I have accordingly written to the Superintendent. May be, I shall get some information tomorrow at Parade.

5th October 1942

Great excitement last night. I was roused about 2 a.m. with a start by Zohra shouting through my grating that there was a snake near the control watch and she couldn't get past it. At first I was disinclined to leave my bed, but Zohra's excitement communicated itself to me and made me get up.

I flashed on my torch and saw one of those grey, thin, poisonous snakes; this one was about a yard in length and was lying against the wall outside the barrack almost opposite to my bed. We suggested informing the sentry on duty so that he might come in and kill the snake, but in spite of the efforts of both the wardresses he refused to inform the matron or take any action. The snake remained in the same position from 3 to 3.45 a.m. but the wardresses were far too scared to kill it and the sentry did not think it worthwhile. As we were locked in, it was not possible for us to do anything. Finally the snake disappeared from view—I do not know where it went, because the line of vision from my grating is limited. I wondered what would happen if anybody were unfortunately bitten.

By the time the wardresses and the sentry decided to give the alarm, the matron was roused and dressed, the key taken possession of from the main gate and the female prison opened—the victim would most probably be singing with the angels. It's a comforting thought.

6th October 1942

This morning the crisp, cool air was delightful and I had to wear my warm dressing-gown for a while.

Most of my time since yesterday has been spent in cleaning the 'political baby' and sewing clothes for it. The dirt came off in layers—it seems incredible how any woman can allow her child to get into such a condition.

Ranjit has sent us some seeds and cuttings. The garden he started in his barrack last year is still flourishing and he brought me a bunch of lovely nasturtiums at our last interview. The soil of our yard is very stony, so the matron has offered to get us a few flower pots and boxes in which we can sow our seeds. The girls are excited.

There has been an atmosphere of extreme depression and quite a bit of weeping and wailing the last few days as the matron has transferred her favour from one convict orderly to another. This sort of thing always amazes me. For months on end one convict orderly will have the ear of the matron to such an extent that her word in all matters regarding the prisoners is law; she acts as a spy for the matron, who in turn favours her with extra food, tobacco, and odd articles of clothing and even money (though this we are not supposed to know). Then suddenly for no apparent reason, the woman is thrown out of favour and her rival given her place.

This leads not only to quarrels and unpleasantness but is the main cause of jail intrigues.

7th October 1942

It was so cool towards morning that we should all have been glad of blankets. My thin shawl proved quite inadequate and I had to curl up into a knot to keep my toes warm!

There is a general cleaning up going on today in preparation of the annual inspection by the Inspector General of Prisons known in prison language as the 'Jandeli' which is expected any moment, as the I.G. is due in Allahabad tomorrow in connection with some other work and may pop in if he feels like it. Actually, this place can do with a bit of cleaning up. I have never seen this part of the jail quite so dirty as it now is.

One point in favour of the former matron was her attitude towards dirt. Everything was kept in a spotless condition and even our barrack which is crumbling to pieces very rapidly and is not easy to keep clean, was as shining as circumstances would permit and the gratings were polished and the beams in the ceiling cleaned twice a week.

Now things are allowed to drift and apparently, no one minds very much. Once in a while I send good old Naraini up to the ceiling and she brings down all the cobwebs and the accumulated dust, but in a few days everything is as it was.

The mice in the barrack are increasing and becoming a nuisance but the frogs have at last departed.

This morning little Jamni came back from school and was rushing off to her mother when the wardress enquired what the matter was. She had come here to ask for tobacco! The child is quite an addict and she as well as the other kids, some even younger than herself, cannot get on without their daily ration! It is awful and the matron seems quite unable to stop it. All these children have decayed teeth from the age of three years and are like dope fiends.

It's a great shame.

The whole trouble is that no discipline is observed. The matron knows that every woman has money hidden away with which she buys tobacco and other things through the wardresses—she knows the women barter away their oil and soap for tobacco, supari etc., and yet no action is taken.

The convicts know that nothing will be done and act accordingly. Even in the matter of all the perverse sexuality that goes on, the official attitude is quite amazing. The wardresses are the worst culprits in this matter as they aid and abet it in every way possible. Until the right type of women are engaged in this capacity and the matron is a person fully qualified for her job—no real change can be expected.

Three new books from home—Lin Yutang's new novel 'A Leaf in the Storm' and two others.

8th October 1942

The Inspector General came along at three this afternoon and spent exactly three and a half minutes in our barrack. He seemed to be in a jovial mood and repeated twice with emphasis—'I am glad to know you are well!' After his departure the jail relaxed. The matron lay exhausted on my bed and the relative of the South African general, Mrs Bothaju, who was hungry and in reminiscent mood, entertained us with stories of her life and conquests in return for a cup of tea and a slice of bread.

There was some trouble in the prison dairy, so no milk was forthcoming until 6.30 p.m. and lock-up was consequently delayed. The evenings are beginning to draw in early and the half hour before lock-up is pleasant.

For several days American planes have been circling over the jail, as part of their general patrolling, which I am told, goes as far afield as Gaya. They look beautiful at night—like meteors among the stars and the tiny red and green lights flash like jewels even from that great height.

9th October 1942

Had a good night. Matron tells me Lekha and I have permission to interview Ranjit tomorrow. I am so excited. He had applied for this interview before leaving Bombay. The government machinery doesn't seem to have a sense of humour! However, we shall be thankful for the interview.

10th October 1942

Lekha and I interviewed Ranjit. Found him looking bright in spite of the continuation of his foot trouble.

It was good to see him again but how unsatisfying a prison interview is.

11th October 1942

There was a terrific row last night in the other barrack between Bhagwandei and Naraini. Beginning over quite a trivial matter, it rapidly assumed gigantic proportions and not only were voices raised to their maximum capacity but the air was made foul with the most disgusting and hair-raising abuse.

This sort of thing occurs from time to time and is most distressing—I have been reluctantly obliged to bring it to the notice of the matron and have asked that only one habitual convict should be locked up in the political barrack. As Bhagwandei is a C.O. there is no need for Naraini, an ordinary convict, to be there as well. It is usually Naraini who starts these quarrels, but she gets the worst of it eventually.

There was an attempted escape from the men's jail last night.

The poor wretch had almost finished a five-year sentence and was due for release in two months. He is suffering from T.B. Now, I suppose, he will be tried and convicted to another year's imprisonment.

12th October 1942

There was no Parade today as it is Id.

Last night the white ants ate through our fruit basket and demolished half an apple and part of a pomelo.

13th October 1942

The political baby is becoming more and more adorable every day. She thrives in jail and has become a part of our lives. We shall miss her when her mother is released.

14th October 1942

Sent some books to Ranjit. He is somewhere on the other side of the wall and yet how far away. I have such a longing to see and speak to him.

I am in a rather disreputable condition owing to an attack of neuritis. Two of my saris have been sent as a concession to the jail dhobi and have been with him for ten days and the two I wear are now coffee-coloured and will not look white in spite of my best efforts. One of the things I most dislike in prison is the lack of fresh clean clothing. However much soap I use, the clothes are always just short of being clean. Motto—don't wear white in jail!

15th October 1942

Life goes on as usual.

Poor Lekha has five hard glands under her right armpit again. They are not giving much trouble so far but may develop. I am tired of the jail treatment which seldom cures any ill. This morning 'Bilaso Mai' suggested doctoring the glands by massaging some part of the side. Lekha accepted and she has done it. Whether it will cure I can't say, but Bilaso certainly knows the art of massage. 'Bilaso Mai' is a rather wonderful old lady. She is a wardress and has been in for eight years. She has a very sweet face framed in white hair which she screws into a bun. She gives the impression of being very quiet and calm, but I have heard her talking vivaciously to those whom she likes. She is the most obliging woman here and is always willing to help and has a generous heart. I constantly see her sharing her food and anything else she has, with those who are less fortunate. She adores animals and catches and tames baby parrots and squirrels.

Ranjit has sent me some new books. They look delightful.

We were weighed today. Since arrival Lekha has lost four pounds and I have lost six! Indu is steady, but that means nothing, she is already below par and cannot afford to lose anything.

16th October 1942

My loss of weight has alarmed me a little. From today I have decided to have some sort of meal at night. I cannot afford milk as I am already using up my ration money (nine annas daily). It has to suffice for several of the wants of the other barrack as well, and goes round with difficulty. Matron tells me that three more people have been raised to the twelve annas status namely—first class—Tandonji, Rai Amarnath and Purnima.

Discussing Lin Yutang's new book last evening, Lekha announced that as a child she had been a

Buddhist, but that now, while still retaining her admiration for the precepts of that religion, she had come back to the fold of her ancestors! My children are certainly not dull!

17th October 1942

Ramkali's young son who is only sixteen has been released. This news has come as a great relief to her. She was worrying about him a great deal.

18th October 1942: Vijaya Dashmi

We observed Dussehra by inviting the other barrack to lunch. It was quite a success. 'The ancient one' was in her element and was specially delighted when I produced some dahi for her. She immediately announced that my foresight was due to the fact that I was married to a Konkani. She herself claims descent from the Konkan but goodness knows how she discovered Ranjit's ancestry!

The convicts begged to be allowed to celebrate Dussehra and matron allowed them to sing and dance. I was amazed to find so much talent. Most of the songs and dances had a touch of vulgarity in them as was only natural, but many of the girls have fine voices. I was quite taken aback when 'Bilaso Mai' was asked to dance. She is over fifty and doesn't give one the impression of being interested in the lighter side of life. She did a *dance du ventre* exceedingly well. She must have been better in her youth. Obviously she should have been in the *Follies Bergeres*. She is wasted in prison!

22nd October 1942

The Civil Surgeon came to see Indira today. He has been asked to see her and report on her health to Government.

This afternoon another 'political' came in. She is the wife of one of the Congress workers in Barokhar which is part of Ranjit's constituency. She has been in before and is a nice girl, a Harijan named Dubashi.

A crisis arose just before lock-up when the 'ancient one' discovered that the new arrival was an untouchable and was to occupy the bed next to hers! She came out in her true colours then and I was thankful the others at last had a chance of seeing her as she is and not under the cloak with which she has so far tried to conceal herself. She has been well snubbed by everybody and the result has been complete quiet in the other barrack since lock-up. It seems almost too good to be true. I am afraid it won't last and she will burst forth into her usual quotations and verses by tomorrow morning.

24th October 1942

Rita's thirteenth birthday. This is the third time I have been away from her on this day. The first was in 1933 on her third birthday when she was in Poona and I was in the Lucknow Central Prison—then in 1938 when I was in London, and today we are in the same town and yet so far apart.

The old lady and Kalavati were tried today and sentenced to three months each.

25th October 1942

The Superintendent has given me no reply yet regarding regular interviews between husband and wife in jail. It is a fortnight since my last interview with Ranjit and I am beginning to want another.

The greatest burden of prison life is having to live with a set of people to whom one cannot even speak…'for a crowd is not company and faces are but a gallery of pictures and talk but a tinkling cymbal where there is no love.' I would change the last word to 'understanding.' I have been acutely conscious of the wisdom of Bacon's saying the last few weeks and the need to talk and be understood is urgent. An interview with Ranjit however brief, will do me good. But why should the authorities hurry about it!

26th October 1942

Parade. The Superintendent hedged about as usual when I asked him about an interview with Ranjit. Finally he announced: 'I shall let you and Lekha have alternate interviews once a fortnight.' Well—that's something.

29th October 1942

On enquiry I find the Superintendent has again referred the interview question to the District Magistrate. This is how things go on, backwards and forwards, and one can never find out where one stands.

Everything continues as usual.

30th October 1942

Lekha is in better health now and in better spirits although the glands persist.

Janki went to the District Jail today where her case is being heard. It is to continue tomorrow. Last night planes kept circling over the barrack from early evening until 3 a.m. The last lot came in formation and I got up to look at them. There seemed to be about five but it was too dark to distinguish clearly. I wonder what this activity means and whether it is in any way connected with the bombing of Chittagong which took place recently.

31st October 1942

While we were having our tea this morning at about 8.30 a.m. the matron sent a note to say that Lekha and I would have an interview with Ranjit and Indira with Feroze at 9.30. The interview has done Lekha good. I hate meeting Ranjit in a crowd.

I forget all the things I had planned to say and the lack of privacy upsets me.

We have a few pots of flowers—poor specimens, but still flowers. It is wonderful what a difference they make to our tempers and surroundings. Ranjit's garden on the other side is flourishing and is a great help to him. His barrack like the rest of this jail is a crowded and unpleasant one.

1st November 1942

Last night I had just put out my light about 11.20 when the outer gate was banged and matron's voice announced that a prisoner was being brought in. We were all worked up and Purnima and Indu were so excited that they got out of bed. The new arrival turned out to be Chinta Malaviya. She came in full of excited talk and announced that a friend of hers had also been arrested and was coming. Meanwhile a bed was prepared for her and the matron left.

She was back in ten minutes with another girl—Vimla Varma. Both are university students. This is the biggest experience of their lives. Today they rushed around the jail and tried to get into conversation with the habitual prisoners and were horrified to discover that most of them were murderesses!

2nd November 1942

The Superintendent told me at Parade this morning that all husbands and wives in the same jail would be permitted to interview each other once each fortnight for half an hour.

7th November 1942

Nothing special has happened except that I am very homesick for the children.

Purnima has given the whole barrack red glass bangles. We look quite gay.

9th November 1942

Last evening before lock-up we had a little Diwali Puja out in the yard and put a few lights in our barracks and outside on the wall.

The Superintendent arrived for Parade before we were ready. He comes earlier each time and causes us a good deal of inconvenience. It is not possible for six people, who have to share one lavatory and tap to be ready at the crack of dawn. I have asked that in future Parade should not take place before 8.30 a.m.

The weather is treacherous these days. Cold after 10 p.m. right up to 7 or 8 a.m. and then gradually getting quite hot during the day. Our barrack which all these days has been open to the sun and wind and rain, has suddenly been swathed in thick jute curtains which are kept down all day and night.

10th November 1942

Bhaiya Duj today.

How many anniversaries of this day I have spent apart from Bhai. Being in jail one has so much time for retrospection and the last day or two I have been very vividly reminded of my childhood days and all the later period from adolescence onwards when Bhai has played such an important part in my life.

Out of the many good things fate gave me at my birth, one of the best was surely my brother. To have known and loved him and been so near to him would have been ample justification for having being born. In a few days it will be his birthday—

another birthday spent in prison. So many good years of his life wasted—I feel very rebellious when I think of all he has had to go through.

12th November 1942

All things considered the days are passing quicker than I thought they would. I think it is because I have Lekha and Indu with me. Their presence is a big moral support to me. Absence of news about Bhai is very disturbing, and the lack of war and other political news continues to irritate me.

18th November 1942

It is several days since I was in the mood to write.

I can't understand why I am such a creature of moods and tenses. I see other people around me, placidly accepting life as it comes to them. If things go against their wishes they put it down to their own bad luck and resign themselves to the inevitable. But with me it is not like this. There seems to be a volcano inside me which is always on the point of eruption and which does erupt too, very much oftener than is desirable. I chafe and fret at my surroundings—at my helplessness at the various pinpricks which are part of life in prison. I can never get used to the state of affairs here nor can I settle down in a resigned mood to take things as they come. Well, *tant pis pour moi!*

I had been eagerly looking forward to seeing Ranjit on the 14th. It was Bhai's birthday and altogether I was in a happy mood. The interview was due at 9 a.m. but owing to the usual slackness of prison officials, Ranjit was only informed at 8.35 and so sent word that he could not come to the office until ten.

About 9.15 a whisper reached me that Rita had come to the jail in the hope of getting a word with me as something serious had occurred at home for which my advice was needed. I expected to get a glimpse of her at the gate and never dreamt that special permission would be required for this.

On reaching the office I asked the Superintendent if I might see her. It was referred by phone to the District Magistrate and curtly turned down.

Meanwhile, my feelings got the better of me. The desire to see Rita and hold her for a moment in my arms overwhelmed me. I hated the thought of the poor child coming all these miles in distress of mind and being told to go right back—I was on the point of breaking down when in walked Ranjit—happy and full of spirits. 'Hello old girl! What's wrong—bad news from home?' were his first words. He came and put his arm round me and I collapsed! However, I pulled myself up in a minute and told him, and he flared up—'Do you mean to tell me you actually asked for permission to see Rita? Haven't I told you again and again that we cannot seek favours from these petty gauleiters who are placed in authority over us. You mustn't let your feelings get the better of you. You are much too big a person, my dear girl, to ask favours from anybody. There is no room in this struggle for softness or favours. Pull yourself up.' And much more which need not be put down here, although various officials passing in and out of the office heard and, in their hearts, rejoiced.

It is amazing how much goodwill there is for the cause even in circles where one would least expect to find it. Well, the interview wasn't what it should have been. I was upset and ashamed of my temporary weakness and Ranjit was annoyed though he was very sweet to me.

19th November 1942

The matron was away from Saturday to Tuesday owing to her husband's operation and Mrs Bothaju flung her weight about in the usual way. That woman is a regular snake, literally crawls on her belly when she wants anything from the politicals, and then she suddenly tries to curry favour with the matron by carrying imaginary tales about us. If I bully her she is at my feet, but if I try and treat her like a human being, she wants to sit on me. She is the only instance I know of a person whose exterior is so exactly the right frame for what is within. Her thoughts are the exact ebony colour of her complexion!

Matron has informed us today that four politicals are expected from Rewa—they will share our barrack! God help us!

20th November 1942

Yesterday was Indira's 25th birthday. She had her fortnightly interview with Feroze and came back from the office looking very happy. In the afternoon Purnima invited us all to tea on her side of the barrack and we had quite a good time.

The Rewa ladies have not materialized so far. They are expected any minute.

A new and sudden development took place today when we heard that the matron would be leaving us owing to the appointment of a new matron by the Inspector General.

The new lady is a local doctor. Everybody has been thoroughly miserable and the poor matron is feeling it as she had applied for the post and has been turned down in a very unfair manner.

27th November 1942

The Rewa ladies arrived yesterday afternoon. Four of them with two little girls aged seven and two. They came by lorry having left their belongings behind and without any bedding. They say the Rewa jail authorities gave them no time to prepare. They have spent the whole day complaining of the hardships that they are having to undergo. One of the ladies is apparently well-known to the police for activities not political and is thoroughly disliked by her companions—but thereby hangs a tale! Mahadevi and Ramkali from the other barrack have joined up with me and will cook and eat in my kitchen from tomorrow.

Kanti Sharga—a B.A. student of Allahabad turned up yesterday morning at 6 a.m. She was arrested at her hostel at 8 p.m. but refused to leave until daylight. She seems a bright young person.

The girls have been busy 'decorating' our corner of the barrack. Each part has a name. Indu calls hers 'Chimborazo'—Lekha's bit is called 'Bien Venue' because she now has the part formerly occupied by me and which gives a view of the main gate. I am obliged to call my abode 'Wall View' because it's so obvious. In the centre we have an old blue rug which in days long past, used to grace the floor of the children's nursery and which I brought along with me in my bedding. We call the centre space the 'Blue Drawing Room' and it is here we eat our meals and sit and read at night, etc.

Indu and Lekha are both gifted with imagination and the evenings are seldom dull.

They are planning to save up rations and have a party in the 'Blue Drawing Room' soon. The menu is discussed daily with great enthusiasm. They can't decide whether to write it in French or not.

The jail cat named by Indu—Mehitabel—-has had four kittens and Indu and Lekha are quite excited. Our ration of milk now has to be shared with the new arrivals and the mother. I have a feeling that the kittens are going to be a terrible nuisance—but sometimes even a nuisance is welcome in jail—it's a break in the regular monotony.

The girls have a habit of giving names to everything: the lantern, table, bed, even the bottle of hair oil which has recently lost its top, as the result of a fall. It is now referred to as 'Rupert—the headless Earl'. The lantern is 'Lucifer'. I find it very difficult to remember the various names but apparently the girls have no such trouble and get a terrific amount of amusement.

After lock-up they read plays, each taking a part. I am the audience. It is amusing.

The walls of Naini Prison are high and we are well guarded but news reaches us nevertheless. I heard today that when Rita came here she was made to wait in the matron's house. As it was my day for interviewing Ranjit and I had to walk along the road between our section of the jail and main building where the men are housed, it was presumed that the child would get a glimpse of me. Prison authorities live in constant terror of the unexpected and perhaps thought that Rita and I would contact each other in some magic fashion. Anyhow, the old school teacher Mrs Bothaju was sent in to her and the room locked from outside in order to prevent her from coming into the veranda. The child was thoroughly frightened and was quite ill and hysterical when she was allowed to go home. I have been very much annoyed to hear this though nothing really surprises us any more. There is no point in asking the matron—she would only deny it.

28th November 1942

Interview with Ranjit. He has finished translating the 'Ritu Samhara' and read some passages to me. They are beautifully rendered.

4th December 1942

Why do tempers get so easily frayed in our country? Somebody is always sulking—others labouring under an inferiority complex and so on. It just wears one out to watch the faces of people.

There is great excitement as matron has discovered that somebody called an 'overseer' is coming to inspect the jail. Why an overseer should inspect a jail is beyond my understanding. I always thought an overseer was a sort of head man to keep coolies in order. It only shows how one lives and learns.

6th December 1942

I had to invoke the aid of good old Maruti today as I was in a fix. He helped me out however, in his usual decent way and I am duly grateful. He really has a deep understanding of weak mortals.

The old 'un, who had been fasting for three days through sheer temper had a row with me yesterday afternoon and, after I had told her a few home truths, decided to break her fast. The woman is impossible.

8th December 1942

I seem to be in constant trouble over wood and coal—no matter how much I get, dear old Durgi manages to get through it and we are stranded high and dry when it's time to cook the food. It's a problem. Today we have had to curtail our menu simply because of lack of fuel. Too tragic! The atmosphere in the barrack is frigid—several points below zero. Fortunately for me, my grating faces the sun and so I can sit with my back to the world and keep warm. What a life!

9th December 1942

The day before yesterday the Commissioner decided to pop in. It has been perishingly cold the last two mornings. The Superintendent told me at Parade today that the temperature in Allahabad these days is 50 degrees, no wonder my cold bath has ceased to attract me! I wondered why on earth I was enjoying being dirty.

Security prisoners have been classified as first and second class and the third class which only existed in Naini Jail, has been abolished. Apparently the officials here were interpreting the rules to suit themselves. Though what they gained, heaven knows.

10th December 1942

A little while ago—about 9 p.m.—there was a terrific row in the next barrack ending by the ancient one beating her head against the bars until it bled. Zohra and Mrs Solomon, the two wardresses on duty, were so frightened that they could do nothing.

12th December 1942

Today is our interview with Ranjit. It was supposed to take place at 10 o'clock but it is now 10.50 and still no sign of the matron. I wonder why jail officials forget the human element and all the facts of psychology. Just a little thought about things would make life so much more pleasant all round.

19th December 1942: Bakr-Id

I am getting lazy. Even writing a few lines like this has become an effort! All manner of things, have happened since my last entry. The old 'un has gone over to the Habitual Yard. She prefers to stay there and it is certainly a relief to us to have her out of here. I am sorry the poor old thing should be divorced from the few comforts she had here but what can one do with a female of her type.

Ramkali and Mahadevi were released quite dramatically yesterday morning and Kanti in the afternoon.

Today was the matron's birthday.

21st December 1942

Nothing new to report. Life moves in well regulated circles—is it any wonder that headaches are becoming a habit with me?

31st December 1942

I have been getting more and more lazy. We had an interview with Ranjit last Saturday and heard that there was some talk of Lekha's release as the police have nothing incriminating against her. I do not, however, think there is the slightest possibility of this—though I hope the rumour is true for the sake of Tara and Rita. It would mean so much to them to have Lekha at home.

The girls invited Purnima to supper in the Blue Room after lock-up. They have been saving rations for days and planning a meal. Unfortunately our tablecloths have become grey with constant washing and our crockery and cutlery are limited to one plate and one fork each. We have a knife between us—nevertheless we managed to turn out an attractive meal and a change from the usual things we eat.

There have been air raids over Calcutta since the 23rd. Some serious ones. Miss Williams who is a jail visitor came to see us a few days ago armed with masses of roses, chrysanthemums and pansies. She is so human and so full of humour.

Chinta Malaviya was released yesterday on the expiry of her two months.

The old year ends today.

This time last year I was in Cocanada with Lekha and Tara and Rita was spending her holidays in Bombay with Ranjit.

The year before I was in this same barrack and ushered in the new year sitting at my grating looking out into the night. How quickly the years pass and what tragic memories they are leaving behind.

What does 1943 hold for us, I wonder. More sorrow and suffering, or a glimpse of the promised land? Whatever it is I pray we may face the future with courage and dignity. My thoughts turn more than ever to the little ones alone in Anand Bhawan. But I am confident they will conduct themselves worthily and that thought helps.

New Year's Day: 1943

'Friends and loves we have none, nor wealth nor blessed abode
But the hope of the City of God at the other end of the road.
Not for us are content and quiet, and peace of mind.
For we go seeking a City that we shall never find
There is no solace on earth for us—
for such as we—
Who search for a hidden city which we
shall never see.
Only the road and the dawn, the sun,
the wind and the rain,
And the watchfire under the stars and sleep
and the road again.'

We were informed today that 'the Government of India have permitted the members of the Congress

Working Committee to correspond with members of their families on personal and domestic matters only, any such letters addressed to Mrs Pandit and Mrs Indira Gandhi will be delivered and they will be permitted to reply subject to the same restriction about subject matter.'

I cannot understand how any two people who have been in different prisons for six months without any contact with their homes or each other and without news of their families can write to each other on domestic matters. But ours is not to question why.

Occasionally we feed the convict babies. They look forward to it and wash and clean up before coming to us.

I have had a small choldari (tent) put up in front of the barrack which I use as a kitchen. The kids come and watch me cook and help to wash the vegetables, clean the rice and so forth. It is good to see their enjoyment of the food. They are exceedingly polite and never leave without saying Namaste.

I wish there was some better arrangement for the welfare of these unfortunate kids. They never have a chance to turn out good.

Our flowers are looking up. The morning glory is climbing well and there are several deep blue and mauve flowers. We have some pansies and nasturtiums also and a row of cosmos which stand against the wall and look quite pretty. The larkspurs and several other flowers have not done at all well in spite of care from Indu and Lekha. Sometime ago we persuaded the matron to plant a few vegetables and the tomatoes, chillies and dhania are all coming up. Yesterday we picked nearly a dozen really good tomatoes.

Lekha and I do quite a bit of reading together. We are enjoying Plato these days—Lekha lives in the Republic. We also read a good deal of Hindi and some Sanskrit. This is the first time in many years that Lekha and I have been able to do things together. It is strange that we should have to come to jail in order to be near each other. But the world is full of stranger things!

I have been reading Sinclair's 'Dragon's Teeth'. It reminds me of so many stories I heard during my visit to Europe in 1938. Quite a number of our friends were at that time, facing situations very similar to those described in the book. The world today seems to have shrunk and consists of only two groups—those who suffer for an ideal and those who inflict the suffering. It is tragic that in this age of civilization—so-called—the human race should be incapable of adjusting its differences without inflicting sorrow and suffering on each other in such great measure. All these things strike one so much more forcibly in prison where feelings are apt to get tense and where one labours under a sense of helplessness. These constant pilgrimages to prison are, as a rule, deadening, and one cannot undergo the experience again and again without bearing the scars on one's soul. It is only the favoured few whom prison cannot break because their vision and their passion for freedom enables them to soar beyond the locks and bars of jail and no physical restrictions can take away their liberty.

Sitting here I find it very difficult to understand or excuse that group of people which live between two worlds—-the world of conflict for the sake of ideals and that other world which seeks to crush truth and light and beauty and lowers human dignity and makes a mockery of civilization. Such people seem to grow in numbers. Neither the tragedy of their own country nor the terrible world conflict seems to affect them….

'Mourn not the dead who in the cool
earth lie, dust into dust
The cool sweet earth who mothers those
who die, as all men must.
Mourn not your captive comrades who
must dwell, too strong to strive,
Each in his steel-bound coffin of a cell,
buried alive.
But rather mourn that apathetic
throng, the cowed and weak
Who see the world's great sorrow and
it's wrong, and dare not speak.'

A disturbing rumour has reached us that Bapu is going to fast. If only some authentic news were available!

9th February 1943

Today Lekha and I had our fortnightly interview with Ranjit. Heard in the office that Bapu is to begin his fast tomorrow. Ranjit told us that the men are all going to observe a twenty-four-hour fast in sympathy. They are sending a letter to the Superintendent informing him of their decision and asking that no rations may be sent to them. Naturally everybody is distressed.

On my return from the interview we discussed the position and decided to follow the example of the men and have a twenty-four-hour fast. I have drafted a letter to the Superintendent on the lines of the one sent by our men and we have all signed it.

14th February 1943

It is the fifth day of Bapu's fast.

In spite of the severe watch we manage to get news of his condition. The first day we had the fast as planned. In the evening before lock-up we joined together in prayer for a few minutes. For each one of us this is a period of very great strain and suspense.

17th March 1943

I have been unable to write for many days. The atmosphere was tense with anxiety and all our nerves were a little frayed. Thank Heaven, Bapu's fast is over and he is alive and on the road to recovery. As if rejoicing over the event, some of our flowers are coming out. It will be quite gay in a week or two. We certainly need some more colour to cheer us up.

The last few days have been rather anxious ones for me. Apparently the Chinese governess with the children at home is not much good and so many questions keep arising which she cannot cope with. At such times I feel torn in two between my duty to the children and the other duty of serving the country which, in our case, has come to mean long months of imprisonment.

The moment I am away from home, difficulties have a habit of arising from nowhere at all. When I am in the house things move on oiled wheels. It is quite amazing.

21st March 1943

Just heard that I may go home on parole for a few days. Shall leave this morning. I hate leaving Indu and Lekha but it can't be helped. They will have to cook for themselves when I go and will benefit by the experience.

20th April 1943

I have returned to jail after a thirty-day interlude.

Lekha was released during my parole period and I discussed with her the question of joining Wellesley College. She was reluctant to leave India and argued against it. But as Ranjit and I always wanted the girls to have the advantage of the wider vision that education in a free country gives, I pressed my point and told her she would be in a far better position to serve India in a few years with the benefits that an American college and contacts with worthwhile people who are doing things, than in her present condition. It is hard to curb the impatience of eighteen but finally she consented.

Later, I decided that Tara should also go. Ranjit gave his wholehearted support and I cabled friends in the United States to arrange admission.

The reply from the President of Wellesley College came in forty-eight hours: 'Wellesley College proud and pleased to welcome your daughters.' It was a big relief—I have had to go into a great deal of correspondence regarding passports, visas and the necessary sanction for dollar exchange and there was hardly any time to look into matters connected with the house, servants, etc.

I saw the girls off to Bombay yesterday and drove to Naini straight from the station.

The parting was a difficult affair and though we were all very near to tears we would not give in and kept talking of other things. As the train steamed out, the children waved to me and said, 'We shall keep the flag flying, darling, wherever we are. Don't worry—give papa our love when you see him.'

I know we have done right in sending them to the United States. They will have wider opportunities of development and will be well cared for and yet… and yet…America is so terribly far away.

We are now permitted newspapers at our own expense.

21st April 1943

I have settled down much more easily than I had imagined.

After the first few hours it was as if I had come back to where I belonged. Strange how unfamiliar the outside world has become.

I felt, during my parole, like some Rip Van Winkle returning after decades to haunts once familiar but now, alas, quite unrecognizable. The atmosphere was different, the people had changed, one's comrades were behind prison bars—a sense of bitterness and depression was apparent everywhere. One lived under a perpetual strain. Back here I am with my own kind. Life may be restricted but after all physical freedom has come to mean less to most of us than that wider vision which we have acquired and which government regulations and prison bars cannot take away from us. It has been aptly said that those who have striven most passionately for freedom maintain the greatest serenity in their imprisonment. I do not lay claim to belong to this group but at least I can attempt to emulate them as far as I can.

Prison can do strange things to one. Forces over which one has no control seem to be at work all the time. Life becomes suddenly ugly and full of hatred and suspicion. Ernst Toller explains this very clearly in one of his letters from prison. Reading what he says one feels as if it were written of an Indian jail and of the way in which the official machine tries to corrupt them.

First class prisoners are now permitted to sleep out but Indu and Purnima are remaining inside the barrack on account of Vimla who is a second class prisoner. I thought it foolish to make a martyr of myself when my health is so poor and have been sleeping outside. It makes a tremendous difference. The space—the fresh air and above all the stars help one to retain one's sense of values and there is a feeling of calmness which I, at least, never attain inside the barrack.

As usual I do not sleep well, but that is partly due to the fact that I am worrying a little about the girls. They are going to have some difficulty over the American trip. But I am determined to keep calm and develop a new inner strength! And so to bed.

25th April 1943

Sending the girls to America seems to involve endless correspondence. I wonder what the District Magistrate feels about it. It must certainly have added to his work and possibly detracted from his good temper!

It has been hotter the last two days and the first part of the night has been stuffy. I wish Indu would sleep out. After midnight the air is cooler and sleeping under the stars is refreshing provided one gets up before the sweeping begins! Nobody can remain very fresh after that!

The few flowers in the yard have been uprooted and the whole place looks incredibly drab and ugly. The habituals are not permitted to come over to this side at all. Personally I like this arrangement as we have more quiet and all the shouting and quarrels are confined to the other side. The constant noise and abuse are dreadful.

27th April 1943

I am told the men detenues of the first class will be sent to Bareilly in a few days. I hope Ranjit will not be transferred to Bareilly jail. In 1932 this place broke his health completely. It is a notorious place and in his present condition it will immediately affect Ranjit. As the summer comes he grows weaker and has been having trouble with his breathing again—I can't bear him to be in prison. He is so much a child of the wide open spaces.

28th April 1943

Telegram from Bombay—there has been some mismanagement about passports and the matter is delayed—meanwhile a ship is due to sail in a few days. The telegram gives good news to the effect that satisfactory replies have been received from the U.S.A. I can't say exactly what I feel about it all—I do not understand my own feelings. I want the girls to go. It seems in their best interest as far as I have been able to figure it out and yet as the time for their departure approaches my heart is heavy with anxiety and like every mother from the beginning of time, I am torn in two by my desire to ensure the safety and well-being of my children and also to do the best I can for their future. Life is so difficult, so full of the necessity to decide and compromise between things which appear to be of equal importance. I am thankful that Ranjit is in complete agreement regarding the necessity of the children's going abroad.

3rd May 1943

This morning the Superintendent threw a bombshell in the shape of an announcement that Ranjit is to be transferred with other first division prisoners to Bareilly Central Jail tonight. What could I say? Up to now both Ranjit and I were under the impression that he would be allowed to stay on here until arrangements for the girls' departure were complete.

I hate the idea of Bareilly. I am sure Ranjit will be miserable there. He is such a very sensitive person and his surroundings affect him. He is not meant to be in the rough and tumble that is Indian politics. With his wealth of learning and fastidious scholarship, his love of art and of all those finer aspects of life which are understood by so few people, this association day after day with crudeness and ignorance is a process which is breaking him down physically. It is a slow daily sacrifice which can be so much more deadly than some big heroic gesture made in a moment of emotional upheaval. But this is not how our jailors argue. I can only hope for the best and trust that Ranjit's tremendous willpower will help to keep his mind and body fit, and the change will not harm him too much.

His departure from here will leave a gap in my restricted life. It was so comforting to know that he was on the other side of the wall. I am sometimes amazed at this sense of oneness I have with Ranjit and yet how many years we have spent apart.

6th May 1943

My request for a change of rations as prescribed by the Civil Surgeon, Lucknow, has been turned down by the I.G. on the ground that 'the jail rations provide a well-balanced diet,' and that I also have three whole annas per day to spend on any extra articles I may require.

I had asked that instead of the rations being supplied to me I might have a loaf of bread, some butter and some green vegetables everyday. Recently the vegetables sent for our use have been very stale and bad and all the potatoes are rotten. The argument is that prices are high and the best quality cannot be bought.

The three annas referred to by the I.G. are now given to detenues in the first class to supplement their daily rations but since anything we order can only come through the jail contractor, and his prices are several times higher than the already high market rates, our three annas do not go very far. If we try to save them up to buy fruit at the end of the week, we are generally informed that the account has been mislaid by the office and there is no record of what is due to us, or some rule is quoted to show that the money has lapsed. So actually the buying capacity of the three annas allowed to us is not as much as the I.G. imagines.

New rules have been made for security prisoners as follows: (1) First division prisoners may sleep out, and have a fan in their barrack; (2) May have money deposited in the office; (3) Newspapers at their own expense; (4) Write and receive one letter consisting of 500 words per month; (5) They may be permitted the hobby of gardening. The new rules apply to both first and second division prisoners except rule 1 which applies to the first class only.

I would like to know who thought of the 500 words. It is really clever and so like the narrow-minded officials who control our destinies.

It is a hot night but there is a certain amount of peace under the stars. They are always the same—daily trifles do not upset them, and they are not afraid to shine on prisoners. It is soothing to lie looking up at the canopy of the sky—gradually the worries of the day are pushed into some distant corner of one's mind and so one falls off to sleep....
'To sleep...perchance to dream...'

11th May 194

Everyday I make resolutions about writing regularly in my diary. They have all come to nothing. Everything has combined to rob me of my peace of mind.

On the 5th we were sent for to the office and informed that Indu and I would be released next morning and an externment order would be served on us requiring us to proceed to Almora and take up our residence in Khali. We have to live at our own expense and be under the surveillance of the Deputy Commissioner of Almora. Obviously, these terms could not be accepted by us and we refused. Since then, we have heard nothing further of the matter. If Government wants to give us the benefit of a cooler climate, the correct procedure is either to release us and let us go to any hill station we please, or to send us wherever they please as detenues. I have no desire to go to a cooler place while my colleagues are here.

Sometimes news of drastic happenings from other jails comes to us, and of course, the papers give one some indication, though owing to the severe censorship, prison news is not published.

Rules in our prison have been tightened up. There are more frequent searches. The pencils we get from the office must be signed for, notebooks numbered and initialled. When I ask why all this is being done, the reply is that letters are being smuggled out of prison. What is required, of course, is not more frequent searches but a better class of wardresses, more educated and better paid. The easiest thing in prison is to send out a letter. I do not write from personal experience, because my wretched superiority complex never lets me do what others are doing, so I am sometimes saved in spite of myself!

Ranjit was transferred with others including Tandonji.

We heard that there was some trouble in the office owing to Tandonji's luggage. He brought to Naini a crude machine with which he extracts his sugarcane juice everyday. As his diet is very simple and consists mainly of various juices and any odds and ends of fruit which can be obtained, it was necessary that he should be allowed to carry the machine. After some unpleasantness he was permitted to take it.

The very thought of the Bareilly Central Prison

makes me feel upset. It is badly located and is known as one of the worst prisons in this province. When Ranjit was there in 1933 he fell very ill owing to the place being constantly filled up with smoke from a neighbouring factory. It took months of careful nursing after his release to build up his health. The other detenues transferred are also not in very fit condition and Bareilly will not help them.

12th May 1943

No news from Ranjit. Of course, we are not allowed to correspond, but I thought maybe some word would come through.

I had a letter from Bhai today. It took twenty days to arrive. He says the more he thinks about the idea of the girls going to America, the more he feels it is the right thing. He says he can't imagine why the idea didn't strike him!

13th May 1943

Indu and I are being released this morning. I wonder if any order is to be served on us. If so we shall be back here before long.

21st May 1943

Here I am back again in Naini after an eventful week! It was like coming back home and the drabness and dirt and noise were all part of some familiar and well understood life. It was a pleasant surprise to find that I was capable of an immediate adjustment and that my mind was at peace. The pieces of the puzzle fell into place at once, making a complete picture. Even the news that conditions in Bareilly are very bad did not upset me as it ordinarily would have done. I know that Ranjit has the strength of mind to pull through mere physical difficulties and restraints. I only hope his health is not too badly affected.

As we refused to comply with the externment order served on us, a police officer came to the house yesterday to enquire when I would be ready to return to jail. I said any time suited me and he suggested 6 p.m. which I accepted. There was no warrant fortunately for Indu who is in no condition to return to Naini at present as she is down with fever and a very bad cold.

At 6.15 p.m. the city kotwal—a person whose renown had preceded him—arrived with a warrant under Sec. 129 D.I.R. My luggage was sent in a police lorry and I was taken in the kotwal's car—he driving and a deputy of the Intelligence Department by his side. En route he made various comments regarding me and my family, but not meeting with any response he was obliged to concentrate his attention on driving his car which was an ancient vehicle in the last stages of collapse. He is a good representative of British rule in India.

The girls have sailed on the 15th. All this time I had been planning and arranging for them to get away and now when they have left I feel unhappy. The days will be heavy with anxiety until I hear of their safe arrival.

I remember laughing at mother because she was always so anxious when Bhai was on a voyage. And now I behave in exactly the same fashion, even though I have more cause for anxiety than she had, in those far distant peaceful days in the early part of the century.

I was met at the jail gate by beaming faces, and the welcome from the convicts was perfectly sincere.

Purnima and I sat and talked until 9 p.m., then we had some food and retired to our respective beds, she to read and I to gaze up at the stars.

4th June 1943

Have just seen in the 'Leader' a message from Melbourne to the effect that Lekha and Tara have arrived in Australia on their way to the United States. My heart has been so heavy the last few days and in my mind I have been following the girls on their journey.

News from Bareilly is bad. As there is no letter from Ranjit it means only one of two things—either my letter of the 24th has not reached him, or, owing to conditions inside, he is not permitted to write to me.

5th June 1943

The heat had been increasing for three days and finally culminated today in a storm. Hailstones of enormous size filled the yard and smashed the tiles of our barrack and killed our flowers. The whole place was transformed into a magic land of glittering white and became beautiful. It is cool, but as the yard is almost knee-deep in water, shall have to sleep inside.

The weather will give the wardresses an opportunity of evading their rounds. The control watch is out of order, so they will sleep through the night and give a report of 'all well' at unlocking tomorrow morning.

The last two nights we have heard lorries driving past the jail gate—dozens of them. At first no information was forthcoming but gradually we learn that these are military lorries on their way to Calcutta by road.

7th June 1943

I received a packet of what looks like chrysanthemum tea from an unknown Chinese friend. I shall not be able to enjoy it without Ranjit and Bhai. One cannot just drink an exquisite beverage by oneself.

I saw in today's paper a message to the effect that the girls have passed Melbourne.

The news from Bengal is bad. The effects of the Midnapore cyclone are not yet over and now a food crisis seems to be developing. The *Modern Review* predicts a hard time. What a mess everything is in, and those who might be unravelling the tangled skein are behind bars.

The news of the treatment of political prisoners

all over the province is very bad. A deliberate policy of harsh treatment and every sort of humiliation. It makes one forget the Congress creed.

Tragedy. Ramkali's young son aged sixteen who was released some weeks before her, was suddenly taken ill and died of diphtheria within a few hours. The father is in Naini in the men's section and parole was applied for, in the usual manner. But red tape unwinds slowly and death is always in a hurry. The poor boy was dead before orders came through for release. When he was finally let out there was no conveyance and he reached home when the boy had been cremated. He has come back leaving his wife and two young daughters.

11th June 1943

I have been unable to leave my bed for many days and the doctors have been dosing me to no effect.

I am informed that I shall be released on grounds of health.

www.ingramcontent.com/pod-product-compliance
Lightning Source LLC
Chambersburg PA
CBHW051118230426
43667CB00014B/2643